The Fortunate Child

A story of a girl who found the inspiration and courage to champion education for all.

ARCHANA MISHRA

Order this book online at www.trafford.com
or email orders@trafford.com

Most Trafford titles are also available at major online book retailers.

Printed in the United States of America.

ISBN: 978-1-4907-2735-6 (sc)
ISBN: 978-1-4907-2736-3 (hc)
ISBN: 978-1-4907-2737-0 (e)

Library of Congress Control Number: 2014902655

Trafford rev. 04/03/2014

 www.trafford.com
North America & international
toll-free: 1 888 232 4444 (USA & Canada)
fax: 812 355 4082

Education is the most powerful weapon which you can use to change the world.

—Nelson Mandela

This book is dedicated to those who
champion education for all.

Acknowledgements

One day, when I was in the world-bashing mood for every problem in our society, my husband pointed out that I probably didn't even know what I stood for. He asked me to check if there was anything that I truly believed in enough to do something about. I paused, and it didn't take me long to figure it out. Thank you, Ashok Mishra, for being my unconditional supporter.

I shared my thoughts for the book with my dear friend Mariel Combs, and she encouraged me, so I took it further and asked if she could review the first draft. She happily accepted and said, "I love editing." I can't thank you enough, Mariel.

My daughter Shambhavi Mishra was the first person with whom I discussed the idea for my book, and I was impressed by what she came up with, being just twelve years old at that time. She patiently listened to me and helped sort out the story line. I would've been hesitant to move forward if she wasn't around. Her little five-year-old sister Aishani Mishra was always giggling and playing around me, asking if I was writing my book. She never made me feel like I was taking time away from her while writing it.

"Do you think she'll come?" Rohini Kaushik nervously looked at her watch and asked Ajit, her husband.

"I think I should go near the parking lot and direct the traffic." He avoided her gaze and walked away.

She was waiting for a special guest at the opening of her primary school. For the past eighteen months, she'd been consumed with getting it built. It wasn't a big deal by any standard, but for her, it was no less than a paradise, a place of learning for children who had nowhere else to go.

The school was a rectangular building with red brick walls, and white doors and windows. The horseshoe-shaped interior consisted of five classrooms, one common area, two offices, and a beautiful lobby with French windows. It stood like a little resort in the middle of a large parcel of land, giving away the plans for a bigger future. She could see the playground through the front door where she stood waiting expectantly. A few final pieces were being put in place to make sure it was ready that day—ready to be the hub of little people making, breaking and repairing friendships, sharing real and imaginary *facts*, and, without knowing, creating their own destiny.

She looked to her left where a steady stream of people had started to fill in the lobby. Prominent among those were children of all colors and sizes, beaming with excitement and curiosity, and setting the four walls abuzz. A little boy, around six years old, was walking slowly, holding his grandfather's hand. He caught Rohini looking at them and tried to hide behind his grandfather, who gave her a wide grin and bowed in *Namaste*.

She couldn't help but notice how the visitors had made an effort to look their best for the occasion. Almost all little children had thick kohl liners on their already big eyes. Children in India have big eyes, she noted. Lining children's eyes with kohl invokes interesting discussions between both the supporters and objectors of that practice. She grew up watching mothers applying it to their infants' eyes soon after birth. Some did that to "strengthen the child's eyes," and others to "ward off the curse of the evil eye". Either way, it signified the importance mothers placed in that practice, so Rohini was glad to see many kohl-highlighted eyes that day. The parents wore their best outfits as well. Women were wearing the brightest, mostly primary-color saree or *salwar kameez* (loose long shirt and tailored pants), many with intricate thread and beadwork. *Bindi* (bright dot applied in the middle of the forehead), *sindoor* (vermilion powder put in the middle parting of married women's head), glass bangles, and gold (or gold-plated) jewels were worn to suit the occasion. Men wore crisp shirts and trousers or traditional *kurta* pajamas (loose, long shirts and loose-fitting pants) washed in starch for extra firmness. They seemed proud to be there and had the look of a runner going past the finish line—"We finally made it!" So did Rohini.

Even though her cream-color kurta with white embroidery and gray leggings paled against the colorful outfits, Rohini was oozing charm. The look of contentment on her heart-shaped face made her look much younger than thirty-seven. She wore a small crystal *bindi* and a bracelet inherited from her *Dadi* (paternal grandmother) that she'd been saving for a special occasion. Looking at the shadow of her petite body on the ground, she wondered. About everything that had led to this day.

Extraordinary

Rohini, the oldest of four siblings, lived in a fantasy world like many children do—a world inhabited by friends, books, movies, and Mother Nature that operated according to her wishes. Everyone loved her in that world and, in fact, worshipped her very presence. When she fell sick, every single person, known or unknown, related or unrelated, visited her with flowers, chocolates, and books. The possibility of getting everything she desired and yearned for was so enticing, she cherished lingering there until her parents, siblings or other worldly duties dragged her out of it.

Even though the parallel world of reality never matched the abundance of excitement in the other place, she traversed between them as if they were a natural extension of each other. She would stare at the ceiling for transportation, and believed that dreams were not what she saw while sleeping but what didn't let her sleep. Dreaming to become like her *Baba* (paternal grandfather) kept her awake on many nights. He existed through the stories told by his wife Damyanti, her *Dadi*. *Baba* was an extraordinary man who had accomplished great things for himself and others amidst many adversities. The death of both his parents at an early age didn't deter him from getting an education and establishing himself as a great scholar of his generation. *Baba* died when her father was a toddler so she could rely only on *Dadi* for information.

Unlike many of her friends, she was closer to her father, Uday. She connected with him better than her mother, Renu, who was too busy doing motherly things. Managing the housekeeper, the cook, and making sure everything ran efficiently were her key priorities. She was obsessed with having a clean house and multicourse meals to which she had devoted her life. Renu was considered a beautiful woman because of her pale skin, sharp features, big eyes, and thick, long black hair. She only wore saree and had a good taste for what color and designs suited her the most. With coordinated outfits and accessories including *bindis*, bangles, and jewelry, she looked like a model for traditional charm. Surprisingly, she dressed her children in the most modern outfits she could lay her hands on. Rohini and her siblings usually set the trend in fashion, and their friends eagerly attempted to copy them. Uday was a handsome slim, tall, fair-skinned man, and, as Renu would note on several occasions, was one of the most eligible bachelors in his premarital days. They were one of the most handsome families in the neighborhood and, somehow, were entitled to more privileges than others in similar social strata. Fair skin and good looks took people places in their small community, or, as Rohini noted, in India at large. Despite being a country with people of many skin colors, even the parents tended to have a soft corner for their children with less pigment. Strange, but true! She had felt uncomfortable during conversations where adults discussed racism in Western countries based on skin color, and felt like asking them how that was any different from India. She once attempted to question it, but was shot down by a harsh glance from Mr. Mehta, one of her neighbors, who was outraged over his treatment in an Australian café. He was convinced that the waitress served him coffee fifteen minutes later than a white guy, who was sitting at the next table, simply because of the color of his skin.

"But, Mehta Uncle, it could be that you ordered after that man and the waitress was simply taking the coffee from the barista and serving it when it was ready in that sequence."

"Look, Uday, your daughter is quite outspoken. I think you should teach her how to respect elders. When I'm telling you that the Australians treated me badly because they knew I'm from India and my skin is darker, then you must believe me."

"Mr. Mehta, I'm really sorry on her behalf. Rohini, apologize to him and go away. What are you doing here, anyway? Don't you have any homework to do?" Uday said sharply.

"It's OK. She'll learn when she's given the same treatment. But first of all, you have to work very hard and perform well in your studies. It's not like any Tom, Dick, and Harry could go abroad. Take my son for example. As you all know, he has been given a special award for the best performance at work, and his company transferred him to Australia as a result."

He was clearly very proud of his son's overseas transfer and never stopped boasting about how he had moved up in life because of it.

"I now have only one desire—to get my daughter married off in a nice, well-to-do family, so my wife and I could spend our retirement days with our son. Let's see when God listens to my prayers."

"But, Mr. Mehta, weren't you in talks with the family from Kolkata for your daughter's marriage? What happened?" Renu asked curiously.

"Oh, please don't remind me of those scums. They made us travel to Kolkata and spend loads of money on gifts and entertainment, only to turn around and tell us that our daughter is too dark-skinned for their son. I am very angry, but let's face it, who would marry off their good-looking, fair skinned son with my daughter who is dark as a frying pan?"

Rohini burst out laughing at the irony of his words, but immediately ran toward her room before she got reprimanded for insulting the elder again.

Some people's desire to move abroad, particularly to Western countries, and their endless rants about the *rampant racism and prejudice* in those places always intrigued Rohini.

After Mr. Mehta left, Rohini was expecting her father to tell her off for her behavior, but surprisingly, both he and Renu seemed to be in agreement with her, even though they didn't show their support openly.

"Dad, I really am sorry for what I said, but he was . . ."

"I know, he's a strange fellow, but you should refrain from interrupting when adults are talking. Now go finish your homework."

Uday was an active father and hands-on with his children's day-to-day life, despite his busy job as an engineer. He made sure their homework was done, backpacks were ready for school, shoes were shining, and uniforms were ironed the night before. He could have left that up to the housekeeper, but he didn't, which was an extraordinary deviation from other similar households.

Uday's devotion for his children's education was well known among friends and families, and he actively encouraged others to do the same, especially for girls. There were many families who thought educating their girls wasn't a high priority, and he had convinced them to change that attitude.

Not many people knew, however, that he treated his wife like a doormat because she was uneducated. Even though he showered her with material comfort, he seldom gave her due respect. Rohini had often heard him yell at Renu for her lack of intellectual sophistication. She didn't know how to process that dichotomy, so she often chose to ignore it, and focused on the positive aspects of his personality instead.

He was pleasantly different from her friends' fathers, clearly stood out with a great sense of humor, and made anyone laugh anytime, anywhere, about anything. She enjoyed his company, and together they made poems and parodies at the expense of family, friends, and neighbors. Sometimes it went very well, and other times it landed them in trouble. Either way, they had a good time.

Cooking and gardening were another of their shared interests. They had a tradition of treating one day in a week as kitchen day, for experimenting with new desserts. They used to create awful desserts—too mushy or too hard, too sweet or too bland—but they had the best time, learning, eating, and leaving the kitchen behind as if a tornado had gone through it.

On other days, they tended to the family garden, which was more like a jungle of eclectically planted herbs, shrubs, and trees. The list included guavas, mangoes, bananas, roses, dahlias, cacti, sugarcanes, cinnamon, bay leaves, jackfruits, curry leaf trees, *gulmohurs* (flowering tree), onions, tomatoes, eggplants, and many more. Part of their quarter-acre backyard doubled as the community playground for all the children from the neighborhood. Unlike her siblings, Rohini didn't belong in the playground and rarely played with other children. She would climb on one of the *gulmohur* trees and watch passersby on the street or help her father with planting yet another species of flora. Sometimes she would lie on a branch, reflecting on the darker sides of her father, that very few knew about. On other days, she mulled over the big worldly topics that she had overheard while her parents were talking during social gatherings. One of them was the increasing trend of nuclear over the traditional joint-family structure due to a large number of people migrating from their farming roots, seeking jobs in urban centers. Her parents and their peers often talked about the merits and demerits of both and how the new trend was defining their values and the connection with elders. Her own family became part of that shift when Uday left Narayanpur, a small farming village, to pursue higher studies in Kolkata and settled in Bokaro, a small cosmopolitan city developed around a giant steel plant.

Bokaro was the only place Rohini had called home since birth, so she was fascinated by her parents' strong connection to their respective childhood homes in villages that they frequently referred to. They had dual-time contexts—one before and one after moving to Bokaro—and struggled to let go of the romantic notion: *"people, values, relationships, food, and many other things were nicer in our villages."* At the same time, they appreciated their modern, urban life and were convinced that their children, especially the girls, were better off in the new setting.

Despite being a small town in the not-so-progressive state of Jharkand in eastern India, Bokaro was a vibrant and multicultural community. It was mainly due to its residents who moved from all parts of India to work either directly in the steel plant or in the industries supporting it. Free housing, medical care, and utilities came as part of their remuneration package, which made for a comfortable middle-class living. All major religions of India were represented in the tiny city, and food from every region was available and popular, contrary to the usual parochialism of the traditionally settled small towns. Bokaro was also a clean and well-maintained township, with beautiful flowering trees lining up the streets.

The general population was well educated, and they sought high standards for their children's education. This resulted in great schools and extracurricular opportunities. There were cultural and social clubs well supported by the governing body of the steel plant.

The city was well planned and neatly divided into sectors (alphabetical) and streets (numerical), and the housing ranged from single-family homes (*A* type) for higher-level officers to multiplexes for the lower-level employees (*E* type) and many in between. Uday started off as an engineer and moved up the ranks, which meant he was allocated houses in *D*, *C*, and *B* types, depending on his positions. He requested for ground-floor houses each time the new allocation was up, so they always had a garden to tend to.

Gardening time with Uday gave Rohini a chance to ask him about lots of things, such as, his move to the city away from his mother or his father's legacy, but he usually replied with yes or no or switched the topic completely and told her a joke instead. She wondered if he missed his father, or ever thought of what life would have been like growing up with him. She felt sorry for his loss and couldn't comprehend how he managed to study and make big decisions without a role model around. Of course, his mother's determination and strength must have helped him through, but was that enough, considering how little women could do outside the bounds of their home in those days?

Rohini and her family went to Narayanpur each summer and spent time with *Dadi*. It required an overnight journey by train from Bokaro. It was an old village, frozen in ancient times—dominated by caste politics and family feuds. Living in their monoculture characterized by one religion (Hinduism), similar food, language, and values, Narayanpur residents didn't know or care much about other cultures or beliefs. A majority of them had never been to a place that was different from it, so they never articulated its possibility. It was a conservative village ruled by upper-caste men who kept their women mostly hidden in the safe confines of private homes, while the lower-caste men and women toiled in their fields or homes. Girls, regardless of caste or class, were not encouraged to study beyond grade 5 in the village's primary school, which was barely operational. Boys were sent to neighboring villages or small towns for further education. Some chose to come back and help with the farming business, and others moved to the cities for jobs. The girls stayed at home after their allowed education level was reached, and waited to be married. Some ended up being married to the boys in the neighboring villages, while those that got lucky were married to the boys in the cities and moved out of their rural way of life. Her father was one of those men who moved to the city-based school and college, and married her mother from a neighboring village. She got lucky. Or so she thought. In his time, *Baba* was one of the most eminent residents of Narayanpur who tried to change some of the uncharitable characteristics of his community. Despite being an upper-class Brahmin—the highest of four castes in India that dominated the social hierarchy and monopolized the right to education at that time—he dedicated his life to elevating the status of the lower caste and making education accessible for all.

Not everyone saw that as a good thing.

Baba was either revered or loathed for his work, so, depending on who told the story, he was a messiah for the lower caste or a traitor for the rich and the upper caste. Regardless of what they thought about him, when Rohini visited Narayanpur each summer, they treated her like a princess, and occupied themselves with the sole purpose of making her happy. That was because of the 'first family' status maintained by her *Dadi*, which made her the 'first granddaughter'. Moreover, she was a miracle child who came to

7

this world through divine intervention. Her parents had told her how desperate they were to have children, and how they had waited fourteen long years before being blessed with her. One simply can't have a child after fourteen years without some sort of magic.

She never got tired of hearing the stories about her parents' happiness beyond imagination at her birth, and the family astrologer's declaration. The astrologer studied her future and told them she was born to accomplish extraordinary things. They told her she had already done that the day she was born—giving a childless, hopeless couple the gift of parenthood and a reason to live.

Enjoying a special status by virtue of being born after many prayers was great, but she struggled to understand why her parents then went on to have three more children. Shouldn't they have been content with only her, their most precious child, showering her with everything they had? She tolerated her siblings in the absence of an alternative, but wished they went away with a wave of a magic wand when her friends were visiting, or she wanted to watch her favorite television show.

The story of her miraculous arrival was well known, and told several times amongst their friends and relatives.

It was in Narayanpur that Rohini truly enjoyed her status as an out-of-ordinary progeny. She also bonded with *Dadi* during those visits and learned about *Baba* through his legendary stories that her grandmother was only too pleased to tell her. And why wouldn't she? Rohini made the perfect audience. Her favorite was the story of their marriage:

"*Baba* was a scholar and a devotee of *Hanuman* (the monkey God), and just like his lord, he had vowed to remain a bachelor for life. At one of the annual conferences in Varanasi (Hindu holy city), where scholars from all around the world had gathered, my father, your great-grandfather, saw this intelligent, handsome young man. Having spotted the groom for his daughter, he approached him and asked for his hand in the marriage."

Damyanti would say with pride, "But your *Baba* did not want to marry, so he told my father he was wasting his time with him.

Could you guess what my father did?" She would sound chirpy and excited like a teenager.

Rohini loved that moment and waited for her turn to say, "What did he do, *Dadi*?"

"Father saw a *shivalinga* (Lord Shiva's symbol) in the hall, wrapped a *janeu* (a sacred thread) around it, and put fifty-one rupees. That was the part of his contract for my marriage to *Baba*, a committed bachelor."

"Whoa! That's incredible, *Dadi*. What happened then?"

"Oh, what could he do once the divine contract was made, other than surrendering and agreeing to marry me?" She would not stop blushing. Rohini wished she could have been there.

After marriage, *Baba* lived a meaningful, albeit short life, and knew when it was time for him to go. Apparently, he had told his best friend about the date and time of his death, but not his wife. On that day, he asked *Dadi* to make preparations for his daily prayer ritual while he went to bathe in the river, and took his last breath there. He died exactly how he had told his friend he would go, and the ritual *Dadi* prepared for, turned into his funeral. Uday, a toddler at that time, grew up knowing about his father through stories of him told by his mother, brother, and the villagers.

Narayanpur was a village in northern India, comprised of two hundred households of mainly joint families. Its lanes were narrow, and alleyways channel through beautiful traditional houses, some hundreds of years old. That's where the upper-caste families lived. The lower-castes lived in a haphazard cluster of mud and straw houses on the other end far away from the privileged side. The village was surrounded on all sides by farms and orchards owned by its wealthy residents.

Rohini loved Narayanpur, despite its feudal undercurrent. That was the place where she learned about her forefathers and enjoyed a number of things that her life in a metro city didn't provide for. During the two months of their annual stay there, she would keep herself supremely engaged with all things about *Baba*. She used to gather children for story sessions where she told them how great her *Baba* was and how he knew when he was going to die. *Did they know anyone else who could do that?*

She became more mature during each visit and learned different perspectives on matters of social hierarchy, family arrangements, values, and beliefs. In the beginning, she struggled as they weren't aligned with her point of view, but slowly began to understand that those perspectives were formed in their own context. They were not necessarily wrong, just different than hers, and she felt more comfortable with that idea.

After coming back to Bokaro, she had to entertain her friends at school with the stories from Narayanpur. *Who wouldn't want to know about her adventures—roaming around, picking fruits, swimming in the pond, and many great (and not-so-great) weddings they were invited to?* Her experiences were always extraordinary.

She often asked *Dadi* to visit and stay with them in Bokaro and wondered what she would make of the differences and similarities between the two places. The village provided very limited employment opportunities. They included contracting on farms or owning them, or working at a few small home-run businesses to support farming.

Just like Narayanpur, Bokaro provided very limited employment opportunities, either in the steel plant, or the big health-care facility for the employees who worked in the steel plant. All other businesses and services catered to those two giant employers. However, in contrast to her village, Bokaro was an urban melting pot of different regions, religions, classes, and castes, working and living closer with relatively less obvious physical barriers. People mingled more freely, and the undercurrent of prejudice was much more subtle and a non-issue most of the time.

Damyanti was the uncrowned queen of Narayanpur, who not only supported a number of families through farm and house jobs, but also mediated feuds along the caste and class lines. In Bokaro, she would be known as Uday's mother who lives in a village.

Rohini was thrilled to learn about *Dadi's* visit to Bokaro for her gallbladder surgery, and that she was going to stay with them for six months. As soon as she heard the news, she ran to the living room to tell her brothers, ten-year-old Tarun and nine-year-old Deepak, who were playing chess. To her dismay, they didn't share her excitement, but she still proposed a priority listing for taking turns sleeping in *Dadi's* room when she came. They readily accepted her proposal, mainly because they were keen to get back to playing chess. Since there was nothing to argue about, she turned around to leave when her little sister, six-year-old Riya, came running toward her, and said, "I want to sleep with *Dadi* too."

Rohini tried her best to hide her smile and said in a grave voice, "Sure, but she'll sleep in the middle, and we'll be on the other side. OK?" She raised her hand in high five, and Riya obliged. As she walked toward her room and looked at *Dadi's* portrait in the hallway, she remembered their conversation in Narayanpur one summer. They were in the middle of *Baba's* story when Rohini realized she had never seen his photo, so asked for one.

"I do not have any," Damyanti replied plainly.

"What do you mean, you don't have any picture of *Baba*? He was your husband, right?"

"*Beta* (a term of endearment, literally means son), there weren't many cameras around in those days, and he didn't make an effort either. He even refused to have his portrait done when the government offered the service to honor him."

"That is so sad. How will I ever know what he looked like? Tell me, was he more like Dad or Uncle?"

"Neither of them look like him."

"Well, that's going to help me a lot."

Damyanti tried her best to describe him but couldn't satisfy Rohini's curiosity, who kept suggesting he looked exactly like her dad, but she couldn't concur. Rohini just had to be content with knowing who he was and not what he looked like.

She paused and looked at the photo intently.

Many people, including her parents, thought she looked a lot like *Dadi*. Rohini had heard about her grandmother's beauty when she was young; with fair, glowing skin; a tall and skinny build; big eyes; a sharp nose; and long, thick hair. *Dadi* was considered the best looking woman in Narayanpur at that time. Rohini only remembered seeing her in a white cotton or silk saree *without* sindoor, bindi, or glass bangles - a desirable appearance of a widow in India. Gold bangles, and a barren forehead clearly set her apart from the married women. Her diet was pure vegetarian that didn't even allow for garlic and onion, as they are believed to invoke sensual desire.

Dadi may have been an attractive woman in her youth, but old age and lack of physical activity had taken their toll. Rohini would have to be watchful about tummy fat if she was destined to grow older, looking like her.

She couldn't wait to host her grandmother.

Upon her arrival, each night, both sisters headed straight to her room after dinner and schoolwork. They slept with her in the middle, and held her enormous belly from their sides.

"Dad, could I bring food for *Dadi* to the hospital when she goes there for surgery? It's just for four days, and I don't have school for another week. I can take the local bus, please!" Rohini's wish was granted. For a twelve-year-old girl in Bokaro, she had much more freedom to travel on her own, compared to her peers from more conservative families.

Carrying a big lunch box and riding in a bus to visit a patient in the hospital seemed very grown up, and responsible. She was proud to have that responsibility and looked forward to enjoying the perks of uninterrupted, exclusive story sessions with grandmother.

"*Dadi*, why did you live in Narayanpur and not with *Baba* in Mumbai?" Rohini asked while carefully taking the lunch box out of her bag, which she was getting very good at, on day two. It was a multi-tiered lunch box containing a large number of items that changed every day. She loved that moment when the boxes were opened one after the other to reveal their contents. That day, when the last one was opened, *Dadi's* face lit up, seeing *kheer*, her favorite dessert of rice and condensed milk.

"Your mother makes the best *kheer*. Say 'thank you' to her when you go home. Can I eat only that for lunch? I'm not really hungry for anything else today."

"No *kheer* for you until you tell me why *Baba* and you didn't live together in Mumbai."

"Well, someone had to look after the children and the farm, and since he had to run the big place in Mumbai, it was easy to decide who was doing what. Now get me the *kheer*, will you?" It wasn't the best answer she was hoping for, but she handed over the dessert anyway. While *Dadi* relished the food, Rohini's mind was exploding with questions. When she was a little girl, *Baba* seemed larger than life—almost Godlike and perfect. Her friends used to laugh at her when she shared his mystical stories but she didn't care as that was her truth, and she believed in it. However, things were changing as she was growing up.

"Did you go visit him in Mumbai?"

"Mumbai? No, I've never been to that city."

"What? Why not?"

"Too busy looking after the children and farm. Where was the time?" *Dadi* continued. "Not only that, since your grandfather championed the downtrodden in Narayanpur, they waited for him to come home and solve their problems. If I went to Mumbai, he wouldn't have been able to visit as much as he did. He was needed in the village *more* than I was in Mumbai. When he came home, he spent almost all his time listening to their problems, and they expected him to fix everything with the wave of his magic wand. He was a priest, a teacher, a philosopher, a doctor, and everything else for them, but not much help for his family."

"What do you mean?"

"It's simple, isn't it? If you are too much for someone, you would be too little for someone else. He was devoted to his school in Mumbai and his people in Narayanpur, and that didn't leave him enough time for us."

"But, *Dadi*, you always told me how good *Baba* was, and you were happy with him, weren't you?"

13

"Oh, *Beta*, I'm not sure why I'm telling you all this. Yes, he was a good man, and I was happy to be his wife. Now don't fret over this. Great men just do not have enough time for their family. I'm sure Mahatma Gandhi's sons would have a very different view of him as their father compared to the rest of us."

Rohini's mind grappled with the paradox of a great man not being so helpful for his own family. She was looking forward to growing up, but perhaps wasn't too eager to endure the hard landing of facts that comes with the 'growing up' package. She couldn't make peace with the idea of *Baba* being a human with faults and shortcomings. It bothered her to see the blurry, dreamlike stories coming into focus through the lenses of reality.

"I'm confused. In all the stories you told me, he was like a God for poor and unfortunate people. So you hid the fact that he didn't really care for his own family while serving others?"

"No, that's not entirely true, and it's more complex than you think. Oh Lord, I shouldn't have said those things in the first place. You're twelve, and sometimes I forget that. It wasn't that he didn't care for us. He probably assumed we didn't need him as much as the other less-fortunate people did, so he devoted more time to them, which was only fair. Don't you think?"

"*Dadi*, you're right, I am a big twelve years old now, and able to understand complex things. Tell me who he really was? I want to know, so I don't tell tall tales of him and get mocked by my friends anymore."

"Oh, *Beta*, there are no tall tales of him. He was a great soul and did many things for those in need in a very short life of forty-five years. I wasn't as fortunate to spend much time with him, and have cursed myself each day since he passed away. He was needed in this world for much longer, but even God wants good people's company and called him up way sooner."

"Are you ever going to tell me what he really did for people?"

"I'm not sure what else you want to know from me. I've told you many times before that he was a priest, and also ran a school for the less-fortunate children. Would you not say that he did good things?"

"Well, just because he was a priest and a teacher doesn't in itself make him a great man, does it? Those could be simply the jobs that he did well. How was it different from Dad who is an engineer, is good at his job *and* helps a lot of people around him as well?"

"You know, my dear, you are a big girl, but not so big as to demean your heavenly grandfather's legacy. Kids these days think they're smarter than us, the older people. If you ask me, there is no comparison between what your father does and what your grandfather did. Your father likes to please people, and you are confusing it with help. They are not the same things. As I said, you are still a little girl, but the time will come when you'll know that difference and, hopefully, understand who your grandfather truly was. I think it's getting late now. The nurse will kick you out of this place if you stay here any longer. You better pack up the lunch box, dear." *Dadi* smiled at Rohini and waited for a good-bye hug, but that didn't happen. She had pissed off a big twelve-year-old, who was starting to see cracks and crevices in her fantasy world. She no longer planned to be back the next day.

"Dad, could you go to the hospital today? I'm very tired and also have a lot of homework to do before school starts on Monday." She opened the door of her room upstairs and shouted as she saw Uday in the living room downstairs.

"Oh, that's going to be a problem. I'm busy today as I have to take my boss's son for his school interview. Why don't we ask the driver to bring lunch for Mom today? Thanks for reminding me though, I need to speak with your mother about tonight. A few of my colleagues from Delhi are visiting, and I've invited them home to have dinner with us. That means, it's the driver again who brings dinner to the hospital. Your *Dadi* will be upset about not seeing us the whole day, but it is what it is."

Dadi might not have been wrong about her father after all, she thought. His boss's son's interview was more important than bringing food to his own mother in hospital. *Pleasing, not helping, is really what he is into.*

"Never mind, I will go."

"But what about your homework?"

"Don't worry, I'll manage. I'm big enough." She went back to her bedroom and closed the door. Staring at the ceiling for a long time was always quite soothing. Making a mental note of what else to ask *Dadi* while continuing to stare, was even better. She should also make up for the rude exit the day before, and what better way than by bringing a bouquet of flowers from the garden? Wild roses and dahlias were blooming.

"Knock! Knock!" She was wearing her favorite green-and-white polka dot dress and carrying more things than her hands could hold.

"Oh, look at my princess. Come on in, darling. I was waiting for you." She tried to get out of her bed, but the saline drip held her back.

"*Dadi*, what happened? Why do you need that drip?"

"Nothing. I'm a bit dehydrated, so the doctors are injecting some liquid into my system. Tell me, what's for lunch?"

"I got these flowers for you, freshly picked from the garden. Do you like them?"

"I love them, my dear. You're such a special child with the biggest heart I have ever seen. Come here, give me a hug." *Dadi* always felt snug and cuddly.

"Mommy made all your favorite dishes but no *kheer* today, I'm sorry. She ran out of milk, but I got you a cream biscuit." Her wide grin made the loss of *kheer* less painful.

Rohini, as usual, prepared the hospital tray for lunch. She then dug in her bag for a book and a note pad, and said, "*Dadi*, I'll have lunch with you and then do my homework, if that's OK with you."

"Hmm, so no story time after lunch today? In that case, I'll take a nap and you can sit on the bed or on the chair to do your work. Make yourself comfortable."

"Oh, no, no, if you were ready for the story time, so am I, and homework can wait. But could we do it while we eat, please, like now? So tell me about the school in Mumbai because I'm a little confused about what *Baba* did at the temple, and where the school was. I've asked Mom and Dad about it many times, but they just ignore the question."

"Well, to answer your question, he was both a priest and a teacher. He started off as the head priest of a temple in Mumbai built by a rich businessman called Brij Bhushan Singhania, a devotee of Lord Shiva. Your *Baba* was a well-respected Sanskrit scholar at that time and happened to meet with Mr. Singhania at a conference where he talked about the true meaning of religion and its various interpretations. Mr. Singhania was impressed with *Baba's* point of view and asked him to look after his temple. True to himself, he didn't agree straightaway and put down some conditions before accepting the offer. He was familiar with the temple and had seen the vast land surrounding it so asked if he could have a school built on that land. He also asked for the temple to be opened to everyone, not just the privileged few. It was nothing short of a revolutionary idea fifty years ago." *Dadi's* pride in her husband was amazingly palpable, as always.

"So did Mr. Singhania agree to those conditions?"

"Of course, as I said, he liked *Baba* because of his beliefs so giving a parcel of land for a school and keeping the temple doors open for all were not big demands. One must have either the means or the will to do good deeds, and Mr. Singhania had both. I still remember your *Baba's* telegram about that news. I was so happy, I couldn't sleep that night, and, for the first time, I really wanted to go to Mumbai." She looked lost in her thoughts as if trying to relive that moment, but soon recovered. "Anyways, so that's the story."

Rohini was surprised how simple the story was and wondered why her parents ignored her questions. She was also relieved to have her belief in *Baba's* deeds and genius restored. She could have gone on asking questions, but it was time to leave the hospital and go home.

"Alright, *Dadi*, just one more sleep before you are home. If school wasn't starting tomorrow, I would've come along with Dad to pick you up."

"How did the surgery go? Did she make a fuss with the doctors?" Rohini's Uncle, Gopal (her father's elder brother) asked who was visiting them in Bokaro, soon after *Dadi* came home from the hospital.

"Oh, why wouldn't she? Anything to seek attention, right? She gave the doctors a hard time when they went near her to give any kind of injection or medicine, or even just to check her temperature," Uday said casually.

"Ha-ha, funnily enough, that's our mother who loves to tell everyone about her bravery in the face of tragedy. I've grown up hearing bullshit about her great husband as well. Everyone else pales in comparison to his work for the less fortunate people, blah, blah. Oh, is she around?" Gopal looked to his side and, sure enough, Damyanti was sitting in the dining room some ten yards away from them. Nothing surprising came out of his mouth. He had always been cynical about his parents' work and their legacy. Rohini's tender mind had tried to process his sentiments, but couldn't articulate what made him so negative about them. She didn't think her father agreed with his brother's views, but he never stood up to him either, just smiled and nodded along.

Damyanti was making cotton wicks for the local temple in Bokaro, and Rohini and Riya were dipping them in *ghee* (clarified butter).

"*Dadi*, why doesn't Uncle say anything nice about *Baba*? The other day he told me I was a fool to think of him as a great man, and I should stop listening to you as you dream a lot. Actually, he said that's *all* you do. In his view, only a dreamer could think like you do about a man who divided and polarized Narayanpur for his own selfish needs. He said *Baba* was a glory seeker and found ways to get it, regardless of the end result. He also talked a lot about the lower castes in Narayanpur being spoilt. And you know what? Both Mom and Dad were listening to him without a word in opposition. Oh, Riya, why don't you go play outside with the boys?" She didn't want her little sister to be part that conversation. *Dadi* went quiet. She kept making the wicks by tearing off bits from a pile of cotton and stretching them into little spindles. Only faster. Riya left to play outside. Rohini waited for Damyanti's reply, but lost patience, and was about to leave when she spoke.

"Gopal has a bitter tongue, but I don't blame him, since life hasn't always treated him fairly. Growing up having a father but not seeing him enough wasn't the way he wanted to be raised. He was old enough to remember him, but not too old to understand why he wasn't around. By the time he grew up and began to articulate what was going on, it was too late. In fact, his father's death sparked anger, not sorrow in him. As the eldest son, he was supposed to put the first fire on *Baba's* funeral pyre, but he refused to do so. In fact, he ran away into the orchard with his friends just before the ritual started. I was too shattered to do anything about that. Time was running out, and your father, an eighteen-month-old child, was standing in front of the pyre, so the priest gave him the torch and made him preside over the ritual. Thankfully, he was too young to remember anything."

"I'll go get some water. Do you want anything from the kitchen, *Dadi*?" Rohini started fake coughing.

"No, I am fine, and not going to eat or drink while making the wicks. Are you really thirsty or just upset about something I said?"

"I just don't want to hear about how *Baba* was burned on a pyre."

"He wasn't burned, only his physical body was. Hindus believe that upon death, the soul, which truly represents a person, departs, leaving the body with no significance, and it is cremated. His ashes were collected after the cremation, and on the fourth day, the boys, a few elders from Narayanpur, and I went to Varanasi to disperse them in the Ganges. There was a feast on the thirteenth day after the funeral to celebrate his life. On this day, the soul completes its travel through a ghost world and reaches the land of the ancestors.

"According to *Bhagavad Gita* (a Hindu scripture), the soul is a spirit that a sword cannot pierce, the fire cannot burn, the water cannot melt, and the air cannot dry. The soul is free, unbounded, holy, pure, and perfect. The Hindu's goal is to avoid rebirth (reincarnation) so that the individual soul merges with the Supreme Soul and achieves *moksha* ("liberation"). So, my dear, do not lose heart that your grandfather was burned. I am sure he has become one with the Supreme, and free from the cycle of rebirth. He was a great man and wouldn't have needed more births for salvation."

"But why should great people even seek salvation, so as not to be born again? Wouldn't it be better for the world if they keep coming back to continue their good work?"

"*Beta*, as I said, for us, the ultimate goal is to break the cycle of worldly rebirth and become one with the Supreme. But not everyone gets there easily. The immortal soul is continuously born and reborn in any one of *chaurasi lakh yoni* (8,400,000 life forms) until it attains *moksha*."

"But why? I know even our Gods take birth and come to this world from time to time and save us from destructive forces. What about Gautama Buddha? Didn't he take twenty-four births? So why would *Baba* not be reborn to do more good work? I am sure we need more of him in our world, don't we?"

"Yes and no. In the *Gita*, the Lord says that he doesn't actually take birth. He is unborn, although he appears in the material world at various times. Even ordinary beings like you and I do not take birth. Just as God is eternal, so we, being part and parcel of him, are also eternal. Of course, birth is a common, everyday occurrence, but what is that birth really? You, all other living beings, and I are eternal spirit souls, transmigrating from one body to another, one species to another—birth after birth. And in each birth, we forget entirely our previous material identity. Thus, in one life, we may be an Indian and in the next, an American or Australian. In one life, we may be a human being and in the next, an animal or plant. Yes, unborn and eternal we are, but we take birth again and again in the sense that we assume completely new material identities again and again and ultimately attain *moksha*."

"I know a little bit about this from Dad when he reads *Gita* to us sometimes, but I'm confused. I think all good people should seek rebirth, not salvation. We need more of them, not less. Am I allowed to believe that?"

"Of course, sweetie. Hinduism grants absolute and complete freedom of belief and worship. It conceives the whole world as a single family that deifies the one truth, and, therefore, it accepts all forms of beliefs and dismisses labels of distinct religions, which would imply a division of identity. Hence, Hinduism is devoid of the concepts of apostasy, heresy, and blasphemy. These are big words for my little girl, but I'm sure one day you'll learn and understand the true meaning of life and death. Enough lecture for today, don't you think? Oh, I even forgot what we were talking about before I started preaching you about Hinduism."

"Well, we were talking about Uncle, was he OK when you took him to Varanasi to disperse *Baba's* ashes in the Ganges?"

"Yes, I think the reality had sunk in by that time and he was quiet for the entire trip, but he hasn't forgiven his father. According to him, *Baba* was too busy doing good deeds for others at the cost of his own family. And you said he was talking about spoiling the lower castes of Narayanpur, right? That's because most of his time was spent looking after their welfare, which was only fair since they were the most deprived and unfortunate of all. They still are, but at that time, they were not even considered humans by many."

"Yes, I've read about that in our history books."

"I wish history was the only place their stories were found but the truth is far from it, my dear. And you are right, we need more people like *Baba* to make it history. He was a great man. Always remember that, no matter what anyone says to you. I used to squabble with him for his devotion to other people and his mission to educate underprivileged children. In his response, he would tell me that he expected me to rise above my selfish needs. 'Anyone can do that,' he would say to me. 'Anyone can live for themselves and their own family. If all of us thought like you, there would be no hope for the downtrodden. I'm not doing anything extraordinary for them, just giving them an education, which gives them hope for a better future. We, as a society, will not rise if they remain fallen'.

"He was considered unusual in Narayanpur where the upper caste never mixed with the lower caste, let alone regarded them as equal. He never saw any boundaries between human beings based on caste, religion, or other differences. He was a true Hindu who followed the intent of our great religion, if you call it a religion, and didn't interpret the letter of the scriptures for his own good," she continued.

"He earned many enemies within the upper caste, including his extended family, who despised his mingling with the lower caste and untouchable people. Each time during his visit to Narayanpur, he would go to the lower side. You know which side I am talking about, don't you?" Rohini was so engrossed in the story that she could barely hear the question. "You don't?" Damyanti asked again.

"Yes, of course, it's where people like Samraj live." She sure did.

It was turning out to be a day for "big issues" discussion with her grandmother, but that's exactly what she enjoyed the most about their conversations. She learnt more about the class and caste wars during her summer vacations in Narayanpur than she did through books and classrooms in Bokaro.

During her last vacation, she learned about the caste hierarchy as *Dadi* had explained, "The caste system was intended as a division of labor whereby the *Brahmins* were teachers and priests, *Kshatriyas* were the warriors responsible for protecting the society from the enemies, *Vaishyas* were the business people, and the rest of them were called *Shudras*, who were people with labor-intensive and menial jobs such as cobblers, sweepers, washer men, and chamber pot collectors. It wasn't meant to classify them as above or beneath the other, but gradually, a social order took place that ranked them as upper and lower caste, with *Brahmins* at the uppermost level, and *Shudras* the lowest. As that evolution continued, a time came when the upper caste had created a number of barriers and prejudice against the lower caste, and eventually reached a point of not acknowledging them as fellow humans. Today many things are changing for the better, but something that took thousands of years to evolve, will take its own course to be completely eliminated from our society."

"But if more of us thought like *Baba*, it would get better sooner," Rohini quipped.

Damyanti smiled and said, "Absolutely, but it's not easy to do. Take for example, Smaraj, a lower caste, and one of the many families in Narayanpur that *Baba* had taken under his wings.

He had given a part of his farmland that would sustain them for generations if they chose to. He helped them financially and, most importantly, gave them respect and self-confidence. Not everyone was pleased with that arrangement, and Gopal was one of the most vehemently opposed of all."

"Little girl, do me a favor. Do not listen to all that crap that comes out of your *Dadi's* mouth. You'll ruin whatever is still left of your childhood and, worse, become a social activist," her uncle, who was listening to their conversation, walked towards them to warn his niece. He did that all the time, so neither of them paid any attention to what he said, and carried on with their chat.

"I don't see a lot of discrimination among the people in Bokaro, but it's quite stark in this village," Rohini noted.

"Yes, you're right, the urban melting pot makes a big difference. But there is prejudice in every society, albeit for different reasons. Humans are so prone to hierarchy, they can't help but discriminate. Let's do a story about Raghu tonight after dinner, it'll be a nice segue to our discussion today."

"Have you run out of *Baba's* stories?"

"Not at all. This involves him too. Don't worry."

It didn't take long for Rohini to finish dinner that night, and before too long, she was back in her pajamas and ready for the favorite time of her day.

"I'm ready, tell me about Raghu."

"That was the fastest dinner turnaround I have ever witnessed!"

"That's because my dinner is right here, in my hand."

"And you think an apple and some crackers would keep you going all night?"

"No, but an exciting story will. Come on, *Dadi,* start."

"So, this is how it goes. He was a poor Brahmin lad and a relative of my best friend. Since his parents couldn't afford to pay for his education, they asked *Baba* for help, so he accepted him at the school. Raghu went to Mumbai and, within a short time, due to his determination and hard work, became an example for other students. When *Baba* came to Narayanpur that summer, he told me that Raghu was going to take charge of the school sooner than he thought. I immediately reacted and said, 'But he is a *Brahmin*!' He said, 'I know you are surprised by my decision to let a *Brahmin* boy lead while trying to break down the caste and class barriers plaguing our society.' I nodded hesitatingly. He paused, and calmly continued, 'Damyanti, you see, it is my belief against discrimination that is dictating me to let the best person be the leader regardless of their class or caste.'"

"*Baba* was very clear about fairness and equality unlike many people, who get them mixed up. They are not always the same things. Are they, *Dadi*?"

A stunned grandmother looked at her in disbelief and definitely wasn't prepared for what was coming up next.

"You know I have been thinking a lot about Hinduism and reincarnation for a while and wish I were a reborn *Baba*. I really do."

"Do you wish, or you think so?"

"Not sure, could be either or both."

The Lower Side

"OK, kiddos, ready to go to the orchard?"

Rohini woke up to the loving, familiar voice of Samraj calling them to go pick mangoes—one of the many reasons she loved their summer visits to Narayanpur. Even though she wanted to sleep in a little longer, it sounded like too much fun to not hurry up and get ready.

"Samraj, she went to bed really late last night. Let her sleep in today." As soon as Damyanti said that to him, Rohini bolted from her room, and was in front of them within a few seconds.

"I'm ready. Let's go."

"You sure look like an elegant young lady with messed-up hair, an inside-out dress, and a pair of shoes in your hand." Damyanti chuckled.

"Yep, that's for sure. Now this elegant lady will also get her siblings ready to go pick mangoes. Do you mind?" She got defensive.

That was usually the routine in Narayanpur—wake up, go to the family orchard, eat freshly picked mangoes, chew on sugarcane, plunge in the pond, brush teeth with mango sticks, and go back home in the afternoon. Life was better in the village, she often said.

"Dad, I don't know what's going on, but Uncle is screaming at Samraj!" Rohini and Uday were in Damyanti's kitchen garden, planting herbs when Tarun came in, all puffed up.

They went inside and saw Samraj and his wife with their heads held low and Gopal standing akimbo, looking pointedly at them.

"What's going on here?"

"Uday, you keep out of it. OK? You and your *Baba*-loving silly girl shouldn't butt in to my affairs. I need to sort this out once and for all—our great father let these people become so involved in our lives that they have started assuming that they're somehow equal to us." Rohini went over and stood next to Lakshmi, Samraj's wife, who was now weeping and hopelessly trying to hide it.

He continued, "And you would not believe their audacity today. They're here to invite us to their daughter's wedding, at their house. Can you beat that?"

"What's wrong with that? I will go to the wedding with Renu and the children. Give me the invitation." Samraj looked at the floor where the wedding invite was lying, torn into pieces.

Uday picked up the pieces and told Samraj, "I can't see the date and time here anymore, so if you let me know, count us in," and smiled.

"Uday *Beta*, I made a mistake. I swear, this won't happen again. You should not come to the wedding." It was heart wrenching to see Samraj cry with folded hands, begging for forgiveness—forgiveness for inviting his master's family to his daughter's wedding.

"Samraj, please don't embarrass me anymore. You are my family, and your daughter's wedding is as important to me as any of my own children's."

Gopal did not say a word and stomped out of the house, his classic response for being humiliated by his brother. Rohini had seen him do that many times before, and was thankful that *Dadi* was away at the temple, and didn't have to witness the drama.

The wedding day came, and Uday's family was getting ready. Gopal was pacing the courtyard as his children, nineteen-year-old daughter, Usha, and sixteen-year-old son, Vinod, stood there

26

itching to go too, but couldn't dare ask their parents. Their mother was trying to avoid any conversation on that matter, and kept herself hidden throughout the day.

Damyanti, not wanting to escalate the drama, suddenly came up with a bad-knee problem and decided to stay at home. When Rohini and her family were about to leave, they saw the neighbors gathered around the house, gawking at them as if they were watching aliens about to do something out of this world. They asked ridiculous questions too.

"Uday, are you really going to the wedding?"

"Are you going to eat there as well?"

"Of course, we are going to the wedding and will eat there."

"We may be the only upper-caste family to attend a wedding, and have a meal with lower-caste people," Uday turned around and told his children, as they looked surprised by those prying eyes and taunting questions.

The awkwardness of the night didn't stop at those questions. When they arrived at the wedding venue, everyone stood up, and Samraj and his wife came running toward them. They looked obliged. It was embarrassing for Uday, as the guests dropped everything they were doing, to look at them. People started emptying chairs, and bringing drinks and snacks for them.

"Samraj, this is your daughter's wedding, so tell us how we can help too. Please don't treat us this way, or we'll have to leave." Uday finally made his discomfort known. Samraj, his family, and the guests tried their best to behave a little more normally, and eventually, got back to doing more important things.

Rohini had a great night eating delicious food, dancing, and sitting through a long but fascinating marriage ceremony. The bride and groom came to seek her parents' blessings, and looked very pleased with their presence. It was a matter of great pride for Samraj to have the master's family over, and he lost no opportunity to flaunt it. What an unforgettable day! Rohini was definitely going to tell her friends at school about it, with a heavy dose of embellishments and exaggeration. *No harm in doing that!*

Rohini's parents never discussed caste-related matters at home, at least not in front of their children. She could tell they weren't prejudiced unlike her uncle or people in Narayanpur. And then she thought of Pankaj—their housekeeper in Bokaro—barely thirteen, working harder and longer hours than she, of the same age, doing grinding chores that she never had to. He was part of their household, just like every other house in the neighborhood. Most well-to-do, middle-class families had one or more servants. They were young children from poor, uneducated families who were brought to serve in the homes where children's education was a top priority.

"There's something I need to talk to you about." Rohini was standing outside her parents' room early in the morning.

"Do you know what time it is? Can't that wait, sweetheart? Why don't you go back to your room, or see if Samraj is going to the orchard, and get some fresh sugarcane juice for all of us?"

"How could he go to the orchard today? Didn't he just marry off his daughter last night? Please, Mom and Dad, I've been thinking about this all night." She was halfway in the room already.

"I was wondering about Pankaj, and other housekeepers like him, who work at our homes, but never get any education like we do."

"I see. Go get your sister and brothers ready, and we'll go to the orchard to talk about it."

"They're here." Rohini was back in ten minutes with her siblings.

"What made them ready so quickly?"

"The promise of fresh sugarcane juice, and swimming in the pond."

"You're impossible, Rohini. Renu, wake up now. Let's go." Uday shook his wife vigorously, being jealous of her peaceful sleep in the midst of the commotion.

"Santosh will come with you to Bokaro. His father has agreed." Just when they were about to leave, Damyanti came in with a seemingly good news.

"Oh, OK, that sounds good," Uday tried to end the conversation but she continued.

"And he is really young. You could have him for a good few years before moving on."

Moving on? Oh, yes, that universal phenomenon. The families with girls who employed a male housekeeper would let them go once they were older, for the fear of a boy in the house around their young girls. Other families let them go once they reach puberty for the fear of their security—what if they got ideas of robbing or, worse, murdering them for their money? "Those poor souls are really trusted, aren't they?" Rohini said pointedly.

"Well, the deluge of media stories on crimes by housekeepers doesn't really help build that trust," Uday added hurriedly.

"Ma, we are taking kids to the farm to have sugarcane juice. Would you like us to bring some for you?" Renu attempted to take the kids away from the situation.

"Oh, dear, I have promised to make *halva* (a sweet pudding dish made from flour, butter, and sugar) for Usha today. How could I forget that? I better hurry up, or else, you know what she's like." Damyanti started walking toward the door to leave when they saw Usha coming toward them.

"Someone called my name?" she asked, as she came closer.

"Come on in, Usha. *Dadi* was going to make *halva* for you but got a little distracted," Renu apologized.

"What *halva*, Aunty? Wait a second, is there something serious happening?"

"Usha *Didi* ('big sister'), all I asked Dad was why Pankaj didn't go to school like we do, but it seemed like a tough question for him to answer."

"Oh, is that really what's bothering you? Well, if Pankaj starts going to school, who'll do all the work for you guys, huh? He is doing what he's supposed to do, and your parents pay a good sum for that work."

"But, *Didi*, he needs to study! How is he going to get a job otherwise?"

"Rohini, his father is thankful that your parents have employed his son, and he's getting the money to keep his family alive. They won't be able to survive on his work on the farm alone, which is barely enough. You know his mother's sick, and her treatment costs money. Where do you think that's coming from? But don't worry, he'll be back in Narayanpur soon as he's too old to stay in your house. His brother Santosh will be your new housekeeper."

"And we won't let Santosh go to school either?" The burden of reality weighed on Rohini's young shoulders, and it hurt.

"Nothing stops us from teaching Santosh at home. You could help him while he learns other housework." Uday said hurriedly.

"Sure, Dad, thanks for giving me the idea. You're a great man, just like *Baba.*" Rohini replied.

"And thank you for your sarcasm. I know I'm not like him, and please don't try to act older than you are. You have a bright future ahead of you, so you're better off not getting distracted by these issues. We cannot change the world, but can always do our part, albeit very small in the scheme of things. Don't get me wrong. I'm glad you have empathy for the less fortunate, but it's also important to be realistic. Believe me, we're not taking advantage of their poverty. By giving them employment, we are helping out their families whose needs are still very basic—food, clothing, and shelter. I know you understand the difference between equality and fairness. Bringing them to work in our homes while our children go to school is not equality, but paying them for their work and helping them out of dire poverty is definitely not unfair."

"But, I was hoping . . ." She wanted to interject.

"I know you refuse to take this for an answer today, but we might talk about it when you find yourself in our shoes. Now, are we still going to the farm?"

"Can I join you?" Without waiting for an answer, Usha reached out, held Rohini's hand, and pulled her out of the room.

"*Dadi,* are you coming with us, or do you still have to make that *halva* thingy?" Rohini smiled.

Without replying, Damyanti quietly headed for *Baba's* room.

When they reached the farm, workers were cutting sugarcanes in anticipation of their visit. Most of those worker's families had been employed on the farm since *Baba's* time. Some of them were given small parts of the farmland, in addition to the daily rate. Rohini often spoke with them about their families and children, and whether they went to school. They were always too pleased to talk with her. During the conversation, they also shared stories about *Baba* that they had heard from their parents or other villagers.

The boys ran straight into the sugarcane fields, screaming and giggling as the leaf blades cut their hands and other exposed body parts. Riya held Renu's hand and pointed at the pond where she liked to watch the ducks swim. Uday walked toward a big fire pit where two people were cooking fresh cane juice in a giant saucepan to make *jaggery* (coarse brown sugar).

Rohini and Usha found themselves in each other's company.

"I don't understand why you were so upset over Santosh coming to help in your house. I know you think our housekeepers should go to school and not work, but they need to fight hunger before seeking education. You know that Pankaj's father was able to buy some land for farming from the money *Chacha* ("father's younger brother") sent him every month. So, when Pankaj goes back to live with his family, he won't be constantly worried about their next meal." Usha tried to reason with her little cousin.

"But, *Didi*, we should have educated Pankaj, so he could get a job and help his family even more. I can't get over what he must have felt living with us when we went to school, did our homework, and talked about what wanted to be when we grew up. Is it fair that his childhood was cut short, just because he was born in a poor family?"

"Why don't you ask this question to your own mother?"

"What do you mean?"

"Well, I'm sure you know that she's illiterate. What must she feel, working hard to get you all to school, but not being able to help with your homework, or attend parent-teacher meetings without *Chacha*? She told me several times about her wish to be able to read and write, and be a better informed parent at school. I know that her brothers, I mean your uncles, pursued higher education while she and her sisters stayed home and learned how to be perfect ladies for their gentlemen. Ironically, she couldn't get an education because her family was too rich and sophisticated to send their girls to school and let them mingle with the riffraffs. She didn't lose hope and thought she could study after marriage, but *Chacha* didn't show any interest in her education and ignored her when she tried to talk about it."

"I know, Mom has told me all about that. I find it amazing that she listens to Dad's lectures about women's equality through education, without flinching."

"You shouldn't say that about your father. He means well and genuinely believes in education for all. He sends you to the best school in town. My parents often squabble over whether to spend a lot of money on my college education, given my main role after marriage would be to look after the house and, ultimately, children. I'm sure that's not what your parents have planned for you. I think *Chacha* doesn't see the need for your mom's education, since she's living a comfortable life with him already."

"Exactly! That's why he's a hypocrite."

"Girls, would you like to have your sugarcane juice now, or should I get them bottled?" Uday surprised them by suddenly appearing.

Rohini angrily stared at him, and Usha just shrugged her shoulders; she didn't mind either.

"Are you OK, Miss? What's the matter"? As he came closer to her, she started looking down and digged the ground furiously with her toes.

"Yes, I'm fine. Thank you for asking and thank you also, for treating Mom like a doormat," Rohini blurted out.

Usha nervously tried to avoid his gaze and looked up at the trees.

"I'm going to help both Mom and Santosh with reading and writing when we are back in Bokaro, and won't tolerate this injustice anymore. You hear me?"

Uday turned around and walked away quietly, as if he didn't hear anything she said, and came back with two bottles.

"Here's the juice, girls, nice and as fresh as it can get. It's getting quite warm now. Time to gather everyone and head home. What do you think?"

Rohini, infuriated by his calm demeanor, didn't take the bottle and started walking back home. Usha took both and followed her cousin.

Rohini narrowly missed crashing into the front door, as she came in running with fury and full speed.

"*Dadi,* is that *halva* I smell?" The aroma of dessert made even an angry Rohini calm down.

"Yes, darling, it is indeed, but where's your cousin? She wanted some . . . well . . . no she didn't, but I made it anyways, and everyone can have some," Damyanti said, grinning sheepishly.

"Could you please keep some aside for the train ride to Bokaro?"

"Oh, for the train. That's right I'm still in denial about you leaving tomorrow. Let's pretend it isn't happening for a little longer."

"Who's going where?" Usha overheard the last part of their conversation as she walked in.

"No one's going anywhere, and we're going to eat *halva* and drink sugarcane juice," Damyanti said, smiling.

"Hey, *Didi,* after dinner, do you want to hang out at the terrace?" Rohini asked Usha.

"Sure, anything special? Wait, I know, a boy at school?"

"No, I wanted to talk to you about my plans for Mom and Santosh's schooling. I mean homeschooling. I thought about it on my way home."

"You're one boring girl."

"Fine then, you don't have to come."

"I was just kidding. Of course, I'll be there. You're way loaded with serious things at this tender age. It's like you were born an old lady. Wouldn't you agree?"

"Usha, don't give her a hard time. She feels for people who couldn't get an education. What's wrong with that?"

"*Dadi's* right, and I really love thinking about those things. I'm odd. OK, happy now?"

"Very happy."

"Come over at nine. Not a minute late."

"Good Lord." Usha Groaned.

The cousins got together under the calm, starry sky.

"So, here's the deal. They have to be serious students if they want a good future."

"Yikes."

"Do you want to help me or not? Now listen before you interrupt again. They will have backpacks, stationery, timetables, course materials, and other things ready before school starts."

"I'm sure the school has uniforms and a name too."

"Well, do you think we should?"

"I wasn't serious."

"But I am."

A faint stream of random noise was coming from downstairs as if people were listening to them and making fun of Rohini's plan.

"Have you told them what we were going to talk about?"

"Why would I do that? Besides, why would they be interested in it? Do you really believe they want to know?"

"Never mind, how about we call it Nand Kishore Learning Center?"

"Sure. Whatever."

"Please, *Didi;* don't you think naming it after *Baba* would be great?"

"Of course, if it wasn't such a boring name. Call it Better Late than Never Education Center. I'm serious."

"Ha-ha, sure."

"I'll miss you. You're a great cousin."

"We'll miss you too." The cousins hugged each other.

"Why is Uncle pissed off all the time, and why does he dislike me so much?" Rohini asked abruptly.

"Don't take it personally, my dear. His grudges are endless, and no one in the whole world could change that. He has a big chip on his shoulder about living in the village to look after the farm while his younger brother went to the city and became an engineer. He often gets angry with *Dadi* for not taking them to Mumbai to live. Then he moves on to moaning and bitching about *Baba* for his double standards for not taking care of his own children and pretending to be other people's messiah. And, oh, don't forget the slimy low-caste people eating away at his entire existence like white ants. You're not in his good books because you don't hate *Dadi* or *Baba* or the lower-caste citizens of Narayanpur. Do any of his complaints make sense to you?"

"Yes, some do."

"What do you mean?"

"Oops, look at the time. We have been here for hours now, and have to wake up early morning tomorrow. Better go back, *Didi*."

"But tell me why my father's attitude makes sense to you, even partially?"

"I don't have the answer now. Let's leave it for some other day."

"You're weird."

"I am. Thanks for reminding me."

They went downstairs and quietly snuck in their rooms, lest the parents lecture them on their late-night chitchat. They had to wake up early to go to the train station.

It was a tough "wake up, we're getting late" conversation in the morning between the kids and the parents. The girls were sleep-deprived but had no choice and grudgingly woke up.

As Rohini came out of her room to go to the bathroom, she saw a middle-aged man and a young boy standing in the front porch. A small canvas suitcase was at the floor, and the boy was holding a bag close to his chest.

"Lakhu, we were waiting for you. Come on in." Uday, probably knowing the time of their arrival, came out and received them.

"*Beta*, this is Uday sir. Greet him."

"*Namaste*," said the boy with folded hands, in a barely audible voice.

"God bless you. Come inside. We're almost ready, it won't be too long before we leave."

35

"Hmm, sir . . . ah, my wife and daughters are outside, waiting to say good-bye to Santosh."

"Why are they outside? Call them in."

"Thank you! We weren't sure if that would be the right thing. They would very much like to come in and meet with everyone. Santosh, you go inside with sir, and I'll bring your mother and sisters, but you behave yourself. OK?"

The boy nodded yes.

Soon they were inside the veranda where suitcases were being brought out and good-byes said.

"You must be Santosh." Rohini extended her hand to shake his, and scared him. He withdrew and walked a few steps back.

"He is shy now, but will be fine soon," Lakhu said, apologetically.

The boy turned around, hugged his father, and started crying. Everyone else stood still.

"Lakhu, your son will be fine. We will look after him," Uday offered his assurance.

"Yes, of course, forgive us, Sir, for being so emotional. We are letting him go away from us for the first time. That is why. Santosh, hurry up. They're getting late." He pulled himself off his son and made way for them to leave.

"Take care, son," the sobbing mother said softly.

"Look, Riya is here. Where are Tarun and Deepak, sweetie? I hope they haven't started playing hide-and-seek again, and got drenched in the rain. Anyways, I wanted you to say hello to Santosh. He's coming to stay with us," Rohini asked her sister, pointing towards him.

"They are playing hide-and-seek. Upstairs."

"Oh, dear, we are definitely going to be late. Boys, come downstairs," Uday shouted, looking up at the terrace.

"Santosh, this is Riya, my little sister, and we have two naughty brothers."

"Tarun and Deepak?" he said shyly but smiling this time. He looked pleased with the prospect of two boys' company.

"Ooh, I am impressed. You've already memorized their names. You will meet with them soon, that is, if Dad manages to get them

36

downstairs before our train leaves. Oops, I still have to brush my teeth and freshen up. I'll be back in five minutes." She rushed to the bathroom.

"Rohini, you're impossible," her parents said together.

Usha was standing close by, shaking her head, as they were leaving for the train station. Her cousin was adorable.

The Other Side

"Hey, how was your village trip?" Priya, one of her classmates, called her on the phone. Rohini hoped she could just lie in bed, staring at the ceiling and not answering Priya's questions.

"Great, as always. Where did you guys go for the holidays?" Fortunately, she had the cordless phone on speaker, which is always helpful when you prefer to extend the state of inertia.

"I was in Delhi for my cousin's wedding, but only for two weeks. There was so much work for school, my mom didn't want us to fall behind." She always called to deliver stressful news, and this one, as always, made Rohini break the inertia she was loving so far.

"Oh, shoot! I haven't even opened my backpack since the last day of school."

"You're kidding, right?"

"I wish I was."

"There's only one week left till school starts and so much work, you have no idea. Absolutely no idea. Well, I think I may have to call someone else. I had some questions about the history assignment. Well then, talk to you later. Good luck, dear." She hung up as fast as was humanly possible.

As Rohini tried to contemplate a good strategy to manage all that work in a tight time frame, her head started exploding. Not being prepared with homework before the school resumed wasn't going to go down well with her parents and teachers.

Her head was throbbing, not just painfully but with a sound. That sound, though, was coming from the door, not her head. She was delirious.

"I got your snack. Open the door, please." Santosh was outside.

"Go away. I'm not hungry."

"Mom has sent your favorite thing. You are going to be happy, I promise. Please open the door."

"Since when did my mother become your mom?" Rohini was being mean, and she knew it.

"Sorry, I won't call her that again, but please take your snack. You haven't eaten for a while now."

The door opened immediately.

"Why won't you leave me alone? And what is that? Who gave you that notebook and that pen? I don't even like that color."

"Um, Dad, sorry, I mean your father gave these to me. I remember you saying that you were going to teach me how to read and write. So here I am, all set," he said with a wide grin—so wide his teeth and gums looked ready to jump out of his mouth.

"Santosh, today is a very bad day. There is no way I could help you while I've got a big battle of my own. Some other day. Go now. Go!"

"Are you not well?"

"That's none of your business. Go help Mom."

"OK, as you wish, *Didi*." He started walking out.

"Oh, and you can call my parents Mom and Dad. It's fine."

"Sure." He looked back at her, a little puzzled, and walked away.

"And I will start teaching soon. I've got a lot of homework to do first." She waited for him to turn around and show how happy he was, but he didn't, and kept walking downstairs, holding the notebook and pen closely to his heart.

It was a relaxing Sunday, and Rohini was on a mission, now that homework was out of her way.

"Mom, what are you doing in the kitchen so early?"

"I was going to ask you the same question. You look a little restless, *Beta*. Santosh is sleeping in, he had a late night cleaning up after us. Rather than waking him up, I thought of getting started on breakfast preparation. Clever boy that one! He already has a good handle on things, I'm sure within no time, he'll be running this house, and I'll be able to relax, for a change. He's also getting very good at making tea. Talking of which, I was going to make a cuppa for myself. Would you like some too?"

"Thanks, Mom, but you talking about relaxing is nothing short of magic, so to celebrate that breakthrough, let me make some for you today."

"That's very nice of you to offer, but do you even know how to make it?"

"Rohini *Didi*, can I help you make *chai* (Indian spiced tea)? I know how to." Santosh asked, hanging near the kitchen door.

"Of course you do. Mom was telling me how you are taking over the whole house."

"Am I? No, *Didi*, I haven't . . ."

"I was just joking. Come on in. Let's make *chai* and enjoy this special day!"

Rohini's eyes shone as she found herself in the company of the two people she wanted to have a conversation with, and the timing was perfect.

They had a good time together. *Chai* was ready, and Rohini wanted to serve to her mother in a fancy way. She set the tray and asked Santosh to bring flowers from the garden. He ran at a lightning speed and got a bunch within a few seconds. In the meantime, she made buttered toast and served it exactly the way she'd imagined.

"Mom, I've been thinking of starting a school in *Baba's* memory," she said suddenly, looking at both of them.

"Wait a second. Why, how, I mean when . . . when . . . you are still going to school, right?" Renu almost choked while trying to swallow a big gulp of *chai* down her throat.

"Oh, sorry, Mom, I didn't mean to shock you with the news. I just wanted to talk about my plans for helping Santosh to learn to read and write. And also you."

"Good Lord, I'm too old for this, darling. You better leave me out of it. I am managing somehow, and, besides, where's the time? I've been fairly busy, raising four children and entertaining guests. May be Santosh could learn the alphabet and counting if he wants to, when he finds time for it."

"Mom, tell me, didn't you want to go to school just like your brothers? And what do you mean by '*if* Santosh wants to learn and *when* he has the time'? He's never going to suddenly find the time out of the daily routine. As you said, soon enough, he's going to start doing everything."

"Let's be realistic about it. OK? Santosh and I can't afford to be students like you. We all have our roles to play, and we should play them well."

"But, Mom . . ."

"And if it makes you happy to know then, yes, you are right. I did want to go to school like my brothers and, after marriage, I foolishly hoped that your father might help me. Every time I tried to talk to him about my education, he politely ignored the subject, and one day, I insisted that he listened to me. I annoyed the hell out of him by doing that, and he said with absolute clarity that it wouldn't work. He was convinced that my pursuit of education would deter him from fulfilling his own dream. His dream was to help the people of Narayanpur find jobs in Bokaro. He expected me to look after them when they came over and stayed with us for as long as it took them to get a job. He also always argued about why I needed to study, since I wasn't planning to become a career woman anyway. And I agreed, eventually. What else was I supposed to do?"

"But, Mom, it's never too late, and you also have a classmate now," she said, pointing at Santosh, who was starting to ease into a faint smile and sat on the chair, nodding.

"So both of you are my students as of right now. We'll have classes on a flexible basis, and I am the first and only teacher you have for some time. You'll have to finish all your homework and prepare for quarterly and monthly exams with diligence. Any questions?"

"Renu, are we having tea today?" Uday called from his room, which meant, "Are you giving me my tea now or what?"

"Oh, we don't have his tea ready yet. I'll do that right now." Renu quickly dropped her cup in the kitchen sink that still had *chai* in it and started filling the kettle with water.

"Why do you panic so much?"

"You have no idea. Let me do this, please."

"What a bummer! I had something special to show to you."

"What is it? Could it not wait until I made his tea?"

"Do I have a choice?"

"No."

"You've already had tea. That's great! And there I was upstairs, thinking you were busy preparing a big weekend breakfast." Uday wasn't pleased and wasn't going to give Renu any chance to explain. He never did, as per an unspoken rule in their house: *"You have no right to defend yourself."* Rohini yearned for her mom to stand up to him and speak her mind, but Renu had always been too scared—of everything and everyone, and it was infuriating to witness how timid she was.

"Rohini, could you get those rascals out of their beds? They are lazing around at nine. We should go for a walk after I finish my tea," he growled.

"I'll get them ready," Santosh said, eagerly following Rohini, who was fleeing the scene, but not to do what her dad had asked her to.

When they were finally out, walking, Rohini came close to Renu, and as they got a little behind the rest of them, she asked, "Why do you suck up to him all the time? Don't you see how he has destroyed your confidence? That is, if you had any to start with."

"Mind your language. Girls your age shouldn't talk like that with elders, unless that's what they are teaching you at school."

"All the more reason why you should have been to school." She was pushing the envelope.

"Come on, ladies, you're trailing far behind us." Uday turned around.

"Yes, we are taking it easy. You go ahead, we'll meet you soon." Renu waved at Uday, and he continued.

"Look, I'm content with having a kind and generous husband who never says no to any material things I desire, and you're fortunate to have him as father too. What has he not given to all of you, above and beyond his capacity? He sheds his blood and sweat for a better future for his children, and you're telling me I'm being a sucker for putting up with him? What am I to do? Leave him and be on my own? Then what? You know I couldn't survive a day."

"It's true that he's a great father, except when he loses his temper and beats me up, and he's a selfish husband. You are so dependent on him that no matter how he treats you, he would seem to be the best thing to have happened to you. That is why, my dear mother, I keep repeating that you need to get an education, and it's never too late. And tell me, are you really content with him just buying things for you?"

"Well, talking about his anger for a second, let's accept that you are partly to blame for that as well. You do get on his nerves, and leave him with no choice sometimes."

"I can't believe you are saying that. Do you really think I am to blame for his random, violent, and completely disproportionate outbursts?"

"It takes two to tango. That is all I'm saying," Renu said and immediately regretted it. "I'm so sorry. I didn't mean to say you are at fault, but it is not as simple as you think—him getting angry and beating you up without a reason. You know how much he loves you, but his expectations for you are higher than any of his other children. Being the eldest of four siblings means you have to be the best at everything for them to follow. I think he sees a magnified version of your mistakes because you are the role model."

"Being a role model shouldn't be so painful. I'm always the victim of his anger, sudden and irrational most of the time. He blames me for everything that goes wrong in the house. From tiny things like a fused bulb to precious things that go missing, are all my fault, and I get the blame because I'm a role model. Does that make sense to you? It's not fair, Mom."

"But have you noticed how, as soon as his fit is over, he apologizes? He really doesn't have any control over his temper. You should understand that."

"It's impressive how customized his temper is, which seems to explode only on me. Moreover, by the time he apologizes, it is too late. I usually have sore body parts, have peed in front of everyone, and am shaking in fear of something else coming my way. Worst part is seeing my siblings, for whom I'm supposed be role modelling, huddled together in a corner, looking at me with pity and gratitude."

"Gratitude?"

"Of course, they ought to be thankful that I am first in the firing line. Oh, let's not forget our poor housekeepers, first Pankaj and now Santosh, who also receive a great share of his fury. And, by the way, your helplessness while he does that to us doesn't help at all."

"You're being dramatic about it now. I don't remember him beating you in a long time."

"You sound disappointed about not being able to witness the spectacle in a while."

"Shut up now. You're crossing the line."

"Remember the pickle incident?"

"What pickle incident?"

"I was five when that happened, but somehow it feels so fresh—like it was only yesterday. We were playing on the terrace of Geeta Aunty's house where she had left a few jars of gooseberry and lemon pickles for drying in the sun. Suman, her own son, tried to take a lemon from one of the jars. That is all I saw before I was dragged off by Ruby, who wanted to show me her dollhouse. I tried to say the same thing in my defense that night. But Dad got angry and preferred to believe Aunty's version that I had eaten a part of the pickle and thrown the rest in the jar. Before I could explain what had happened, my back was stinging with pain from the wooden stick he hit me with."

"I'm amazed at your memory. Yes, I remember that incident now, but it was such a long time ago. And yes, you peed in your pants. Ha!"

"Yeah, I did, and I'm shocked that you find it funny. Do you see why I remember it so well? I peed because I was so scared, I lost control over my bladder. What was my mistake? Why did he hurt me so much?"

"Why did you eat the pickle?"

"Mom, I did not eat the pickle."

"Well, your dad didn't just guess that. He was told by an adult who came home complaining about it. Geeta said her son had seen you do that. You know how angry your father gets if his family does anything wrong to the neighbors. I'm not saying the punishment was justified for what you did, but, Rohini, you should have asked me for a pickle if you wanted it so bad. We had at least a dozen jars in the kitchen."

"Mom, please trust me! I never ate that pickle. I wasn't even there when that pickle was eaten. I was playing with Ruby."

"OK, I get it now, but why are we digging up such an ancient story about a petty thing?"

"Being beaten for something I never did is not a petty thing. That was the first time I endured violence by my father. It is etched in my memory forever, and I am not being dramatic about it, just sharing my pain with you. I also remember when I came back after changing my soiled clothes, everyone was laughing at my situation. You guys continued to have a good time over Ms. Pissy Pants for long. And of all people, Dad had enjoyed it so much that he started beating me for almost anything since that day. I obviously provided the comic relief, peeing each time. But you know what hurts the most? Your lack of trust, and I know you are still assuming, no, convinced that I stole that bloody pickle."

"How am I supposed to verify that? When Geeta said her son saw you do that, what more did we need to know?"

"What more did you need to know? You needed to trust your own child and ask her if that was true."

"And you were going to tell me the truth?"

"Why do you think I wasn't telling the truth?"

"I don't know, for heaven's sake! Look, you're ruining my day, this one day I thought I should take it easy. I still don't understand why you are clinging to that story. Let go of it and focus on more important things like your studies or what you would like to be in the future. This argument over 'the pickle theft when you were five', will take you nowhere."

"Fine then, I won't ruin it anymore." She started walking back home furiously and then turned around swiftly.

"There is so much more that could ruin your day, but I will keep it with me."

"Let's hear what more you have been keeping in your Pandora's box? Let's sit on the bench and talk. Shall we? People are watching us."

"You won't be able to hear. Forget it."

"No, I won't forget it. You have annoyed me enough today. Get this off your chest as well." Renu was shaking with anger and gestured Rohini to sit down.

They sat on the bench under the banyan tree. The giant tree had always soothed her before, but who knew what was destined that day.

"How would you react to know that my own father tried to violate me, I mean, sexually?"

"Ha, you have some guts to lie, haven't you? Your father has told me everything, as he probably knew you might make up your own story about it one day."

"What do you mean by everything?"

"It happened when I was away to see my sister, didn't it?"

"Yes, and also . . ."

"See, I told you I know everything."

"But how am I lying?"

"You said he violated you, right? But he told me you crawled into his bed and started feeling his privates one night. He said he felt awkward and didn't know how to stop you."

"What the hell? Is that what he said happened?"

"That is what happened. There is no other truth."

"Or you would rather be in denial."

46

"Whatever."

"So I take it as yes. You think I'm lying and you know the truth."

"Do you realize how living in a fantasy world has made you a perpetual liar? Come off it, Rohini, and be with us in reality. Everything will be fine, trust me. There is no harm in accepting you made a mistake, even a gross one like that. As far as we are concerned, we have forgiven you."

"You have forgiven me? For what? For suffering those nights of terror and wondering if I'm the only unfortunate child around? For carrying those scars for the rest of my life? For not being able to talk about it even with my mother who thinks I am at fault?"

"Here's a piece of advice, change yourself or be destined to suffer. Your mind is so contaminated with filthy imaginations, bizarre dreams, and random desires that you have started making things up. Unless you start writing fiction, these qualities aren't going to help you in any way. And listen, please don't show me these crocodile tears." Renu got up and started walking to join the rest of the family. Rohini buried her face in her hands and cried.

A few weeks had passed since the bitter argument between them, but Rohini was still overcome with shock and hurt. Renu, however, behaved as if nothing had happened.

"Priya called half an hour ago, panicking about the science homework. I didn't understand what exactly the problem was, but I think you should call her back," Renu came into her room and said. Rohini didn't look up to answer.

"I didn't see you coming back from your piano lesson tonight. How was it today? Did you get a new teacher for the year? I hope you did. Mrs. Kapoor doesn't have a good reputation as a piano expert," Renu continued, but Rohini pretended to be engrossed in her books and didn't react.

"What's the matter? Are you stressed about the homework as well?"

"My head is hurting. Do you mind leaving me alone?"

"Oh, I better ask Santosh to get you medicine and head balm. Wait."

"That won't be necessary. Thanks a lot for what I am sure is your genuine concern about me. I have a lot of schoolwork to do, if only you could understand what that means. And please close the door behind you."

The door was slammed shut and marked the souring of their relationship for months. Strangely enough, Rohini was as normal with Uday as was possible. He had no reason to guess that anything had changed.

"Mommy, why is *Didi* not talking to you?" Santosh asked Renu when she was supervising him in the kitchen.

"What makes you think she's not talking to me? She's just a little stressed about her schoolwork. That's all. Being in ninth grade is a big deal, you know."

"I see, but she's talking to everyone else normally."

"Hey, just focus on what you need to do and don't poke your nose in everyone else's business. OK?"

"OK."

"I'm not talking to her because she's not agreeing to join the school I planned to run for both of you." Rohini barged in to the kitchen and smiled. She better use her lying prowess now. It was hard, but overcoming the anger and frustration seemed the only way forward.

"I'm ready. When do we start? Should I get my notebook? Mommy, do you have yours?" Santosh was ecstatic, but Renu hadn't change her stance.

"I won't have any time for it. Haven't I told you before?"

"Yes, you have, but that's an excuse. Let's at least try, and if that doesn't work, fine. We won't regret never giving it a go. Please, Mom, it's my dream to see you read and write. I've been very mean to you, and I'm sorry about that, but that's because I really do not understand how you could be content with the way things are."

"When would you find the time out of schoolwork, piano lessons, painting classes, and the other million things you're involved with?" Renu tried to respond politely, but was still resisting the study plan.

"And that is yet another excuse. Don't worry about me. I'll manage all that. You just need to make time for your studies, and I'm sure you will, if you really want to. I'm talking to both of you. Are you listening, Santosh?"

The school started that day with the English and Hindi alphabet. Her students showed interest and followed instructions diligently. They got daily tasks and also studied on weekends. Life was finally good for the three of them.

Rohini was so happy about running her school with real students that she wanted the entire world to know. The only problem was she didn't want them to know that her mother was illiterate.

As time passed, Rohini's school and extracurriculars started to suffer, and Uday started to take notice.

"Where is she?" he asked Renu as soon as she opened the door for him one evening.

"At her piano lesson. Why?"

"I was called by her science teacher today. Do you know your darling daughter is making great progress at school, and has secured a *B* this term? I want to know what's going on."

"She'll be back soon. You freshen up first. Santosh, make a cup of tea for Dad."

Santosh quickly hid his books in the pantry and rushed to make tea lest he get in trouble.

"*Didi* was not well on the day of her science exam," he said as he served tea to Uday.

"Oh, so you're going to advocate for her, huh?"

"No, I was just . . . saying . . ."

"You keep your mouth shut, all right? I know she is distracted and needs to be brought back on track. You just do the housework. I'm saying that to both of you. Renu, you need to hear this too. I've seen her spending a lot of time with you guys lately, and come to think of it, her grades have been falling since that school opening drama took place. I'm not blind, you know."

"I'm sure she'll pick her grades up. You know she is a good student, and responsible too. Don't be harsh on her. She's doing a lot at the moment." Renu wanted to calm him down, dreading his angry outburst for Rohini.

"Exactly! She is doing a lot of *other* things. And what would you know about her grades? She could say anything, and you would believe it. I want her focused on studies and nothing else. All that piano, painting, and creative writing shit have to stop now. She's in ninth grade, and if she screws that up, there is no future for her. No future."

Renu and Santosh slowly walked toward the kitchen and held their breath for what awaited Rohini when she was back.

The phone rang in the living room, and Uday picked it up quickly.

"Hello."

"Hi, Dad."

"Where are you? Weren't you supposed to be home now?"

"Yes, but my piano teacher's housekeeper fell off the stairs and cut her chin. I'm taking her to the hospital."

"Get your ass back here, will you? And may I ask why you, and not your teacher, are taking that servant to hospital?"

"I'm sorry, but you are not to speak with me like that. And I'm going to the hospital because this girl needs my help. My teacher has a baby to take care of. Just in case you've forgotten, she is a widow and has to manage everything on her own. Besides, I have chosen to help, and I don't think that's a crime, unless you have a different definition." She hung up.

He was furious, and couldn't believe his daughter's audacity. It was highly unusual for her to speak up to him. She must be checked before it was too late.

"Renu, you probably heard where she is. I'm surprised at her guts, and I suspect it's that feminist piano teacher influencing her. They seem to be getting along a bit too well. I'm going over to her house to give her a piece of my mind."

"Does it look good for you to do that?" Renu said sheepishly.

"Shut the hell up, you illiterate woman! Leave it up to me to decide what's good and bad. Let me fix that teacher first. And let Rohini come back from the hospital. That girl will either mend her ways or regret this day for the rest of her life. I cannot sit here on my hands, and let her waste my money on her education if all she wants to do is social welfare. I've had enough." He turned around, slammed the door, and left.

Riya and the boys were hiding behind the curtain that parted the living and dining rooms. Renu hauled them upstairs and wondered if that day was going to end in another spectacle of Rohini being beaten up and her siblings witnessing that in shock. She wished she could save her from Uday's fury.

It was around eight in the evening when the door bell rang, but before he could reach the door, Santosh ran over and opened it.

"May I ask why you went to see my piano teacher and misbehaved with her? What wrong has she done to you?" She entered the house furiously and asked Uday, who was halfway to the door.

"Because I'm your father, and I'm the one who pays for your education. I'm sure that gives me the right to fix anything that comes in the way. That feminist shit is contaminating your mind, and I'm asking you to stay away from her. I also know that you are spending a lot more time doing things other than studies, and those have to stop too."

"You have a filthy mind, and you see everyone that way. So you are telling me that I need to obey every rule that you come up with if I want my education to continue? To hell with that."

Uday slapped Rohini so hard that she fell on the floor. Santosh leapt to her rescue, but it was too late.

"To hell with that, huh? OK then, your education ends today. Go get in the kitchen and join your good-for-nothing mother in homemaking. You may need that sooner than you thought." He expected her to answer back and waited for a few seconds.

She didn't say anything, got up, and went in to the kitchen.

"He's such a twisted jerk," she blurted out while washing her face and started crying.

"He may be a jerk, but, *Beta*, he is doing that for your benefit. You know how dedicated he is to your education. Tell me honestly that you are not distracted. I mean, you never got a *B* in science before."

"I'm not going to school tomorrow, so don't make my lunch. One less thing to worry about, I guess."

"Oh, you really think that's going to happen? Wait till dinner time, and he will come, apologizing. Everything will be fine, I am sure."

"Yuck, his apologies! Do they even mean anything? And please don't bother calling me for dinner. I would rather go hungry than have a meal with him tonight."

"Don't be such a thankless daughter. You have much to be grateful for."

"Sure, Mom, sure. But not tonight, please." She left and went in to her room. Staring at the ceiling was still so soothing.

"Rohini, open the door. It's Dad. I'm very sorry for what I said, but it was only for your benefit. Open the door and come have dinner."

Oh, shit!

The school had dwindled since its inception, but Rohini was determined to persevere. She taught Santosh and Renu on an ad hoc basis, and they cooperated and worked hard to learn. After three years of schooling, they were able to read and write, albeit at a very basic level. Santosh learned more and faster than Renu and was very proud of that.

"*Didi*, I made a card for you for your birthday."

"Have you? That's very thoughtful. Thanks."

"Here it is. Please open it."

"But my birthday isn't until next month."

"I know, but you should see your card now."

"Alright then, ah, I see, you have written birthday wishes and signed your name, all in English! I'm very impressed."

"Thank you, and you know what? Mommy couldn't do that. When I asked her to write in English, she got angry at me and said that she preferred to write in Hindi instead." He giggled triumphantly, but suddenly looked worried.

"*Didi*, who will teach us when you go to college in two months?"

"You know, I have been thinking about that too. Maybe the boys might be able to help. I'll talk to them, but if they are not keen, I'm sure you are now able to do it yourself too. I'll also check on it when I come home in the summer."

The Responsible Side

E ven though Rohini was looking forward to life at college in Delhi, when the day came for her to leave Bokaro, she was far from prepared. The thought of leaving the city where she had grown up as a precious, beaten, valued, assaulted, mocked at, and revered child, was overwhelming. Her dad obviously expected her to thrive in the great unknown, and be a role model for her siblings.

The next six years in Delhi were transformative. She grew up to be a confident young woman, better learned and toughened through the life-enriching experiences in boarding. College rewarded her with fun and turmoil—relationships made and changed, rules broken and consequences borne, and two graduate degrees acquired in economics and law.

Back home, the education of her students continued, but not much progress was made since she'd left. She barely succeeded in keeping them on track, but they did their best, given her absence and the competing demands of housework, and three children. To her surprise, Uday had changed his attitude and started helping them, which she thought was the best thing he ever did for her. As expected, it turned out that her brothers weren't so keen on taking up the teacher's role.

After six years and two degrees worth of college, Rohini was ready to take on the world. She started working at a law firm in Delhi, and managed to impress her seniors with her positive energy and hard work, much to the annoyance of her colleagues. Hence, they were pleased to hear about her engagement with a boy living in Mumbai. She herself wasn't too sure about that future, in the beginning.

She had known Ajit since childhood but never thought of him as a future husband. Until her parents suggested that he could be a good match for her, she was too busy being the world's greatest budding lawyer to think about marriage. When they asked her opinion, she said even though she didn't really love Ajit, there was nothing wrong with him.

"You're right, there's nothing wrong with him, and you've known him forever as a friend and a senior at school. I think you should just say yes to the proposal." Renu was on the phone one morning when Rohini was about to leave for work.

"Mom, knowing him as a friend and senior at school is not the same as knowing him as my life partner. I never thought of him that way. Though this proposal makes me think."

"Great, I'm hearing a yes then."

"Mom, don't jump to conclusions."

"You aren't leaving me with an alternative interpretation."

"Look, can we talk about it tomorrow? I'll have some time to think about it. A decision about living with someone for life warrants at least twelve hours of contemplation."

"I'll call you at eight in the morning then, just after breakfast."

"Seriously? What will happen if you stretched it to nine, for example?"

"Nine then, no more negotiation." Renu hung up on her.

Ajit's work in Mumbai was one of his most attractive attributes for Rohini, since she always wanted to go there to be closer to *Baba's* legacy. However, after a few hours of soul searching, her connection with him seemed a little more profound than she initially thought.

She remembered the day when Priya, now her classmate in college, told her that Ajit was going out with her elder sister Sonal.

"Oh, how is that possible? They aren't even from the same caste" was all she could mutter.

"Rohini, how could you say that? I thought you didn't see any barriers between people loving each other. I remember you were so proud of Usha for marrying a low-caste boy against your uncle's wishes. Don't you think Ajit and Sonal are made for each other?"

"Yes, of course they do. I'm sorry about my stupid comment, I was distracted," she said, without meaning it.

For the next few days after that conversation, she spent a lot of time trying to find out how involved they really were and gathered, mostly from the grapevine, that Ajit may not be as keen on Sonal as she was on him. There was hope, she thought, at least until Ajit told her otherwise.

Soon after that news, Ajit came to Delhi for a job interview and called her on the phone to ask if they could meet while he was in town. She took all of two seconds to say yes for a meeting, and when he met her, he went ahead and asked her to join him for dinner. Her jaw dropped.

Even though she was disappointed that Ajit's friends were at the dinner as well, it was a relief not to see Sonal there. The dinner was nice, and Rohini enjoyed the company of her seniors. She also caught Ajit admiringly looking at her a few times. She, of course, didn't mind that at all. Best thing was, she heard the news of Sonal's affair with another boy.

She was lost in her dream about that beautiful night when her mom's phone call woke her up.

"Just checking if it's a definite yes, so I can start the preparations," her mom asked, suddenly sounding chirpy.

"Sure, Mom, whatever it takes to not get your call so early in the morning."

"I knew you wouldn't say no to marry Ajit. After all, you two have always been such good friends and he is perfect in every way. A well-paying job, a great heritage, and he's a Brahmin."

"Mom, wait. You're saying Ajit's perfect because he's also a Brahmin?"

"No, I mean, yes, that counts too. Goodness, why did I have to say that to you? Listen, dear, why are we complicating a simple decision to marry the perfect boy?"

"I'm just questioning the definition of being perfect."

"Rohini, if you're suggesting I'm being biased, aren't you doing the same? If you like him, say yes, regardless of what other things I consider good about him."

"I need some more time."

"How much more?"

"I don't know. I'll call you once I've made up my mind."

"Don't take forever."

"I won't." She hung up with a big sigh.

She called Usha to talk about her predicament.

"Rohini, you have to ask yourself why you're opposing your mother. Is it because of his caste and status? Then aren't you being prejudiced? If you like him enough to accept him as your husband, then go for it. I know sometimes we tend to discriminate when we try to be fair. If your mom thinks he's a good match because of his status, that's not fair, but it shouldn't affect your decision, whatever it may be."

"Thanks, *Didi*, that makes sense," she said quickly, as if that was what she wanted to hear.

"I do like him, but I hadn't realized it until Mom mentioned the marriage. I'm intrigued by the proposal from his family, though. Ajit and I haven't met since a brief dinner a few years ago in Delhi. I'm sure he must have come across many girls since then, who are probably better suited for marriage."

"Have you asked that question yourself? Haven't you met anyone since that time who might be a good match? I know a lot of them would love to be with you. Why didn't you go for one of them? You know the answer, or do I need to say anymore?" Usha chuckled.

"I love you, Cousin, but got to go, getting late for work. Bye!" Rohini put the phone down and did a happy dance before dialing in her mom's number.

"Yes, it makes sense, totally!" She chirped before Renu could say hello.

"Hello, Rohini, is that the good news I've been waiting for?"

"Yes, I'm happy to consider marrying the perfect Brahmin boy."

"I'm so glad, my dear. You know you two are the match made in heaven."

"Just to make it clear, I'm not marrying him because he's well-off and a Brahmin, but despite it."

"OK, got it. As long as you say yes, I'm not fussed about why you agreed."

"Great, Mom. I'm really getting late for work. Talk to you soon. Bye."

"Rohini ma'am, you've got a letter from Mumbai." The office boy came to her desk and delivered an envelope.

"Dear Rohini,

I hope you are well and happy doing what you always wanted to do— seek justice for all.

I'm not sure if you were expecting to hear from me, but I thought it made sense to touch base, now that we're going to be more than what we have been for years.

My mom called me last week and said that you've agreed to my marriage proposal. You may think I'm a coward for not asking you directly, and you won't be wrong. I wasn't sure if you considered me worthy of becoming your life partner, and I was hesitant to put you in a tight spot by asking, or worse, hearing your outright rejection.

Rohini, I've never said this to you before, but as long as I remember, you were always the person I connected with from the bottom of my heart. You always charmed me without the slightest effort. I wanted to be close to you but didn't want to be overbearing or try too hard to please you.

You know how off-putting that can be, right? (I've heard you say that too many times to make the same mistake.)

You have no idea how happy I am to know that you would like to spend the rest of your life with me. I don't have words to thank you for giving me the gift of your partnership. I shall always cherish the trust you have put in me and our relationship, which has yet to blossom. Let's celebrate the beginning.

Forever yours,
Ajit Kaushik
(P.S. Can I call you sometime? I have your phone number.)"

Rohini read the letter at least four times in quick succession and then many more times during the day. She couldn't believe Ajit was thanking her for accepting his proposal. She also looked at his name written in full—something she didn't remember noticing before. Ajit Kaushik, that meant she could become Rohini Kaushik if she wanted to, and it sounded kind of romantic. *Rohini Kaushik.*

They became closer and more open about their future together after that letter, met a number of times, and grew more confident that they were going to be in a happy marriage. And just like that, in the eight months of their engagement, they transitioned from being great mates to soul mates.

On a fine summer day, they tied the knot in a simple, traditional, and beautiful ceremony in their common hometown Bokaro. Uday surprised her by inviting Raghu, *Baba's* favorite student, from Mumbai, who performed the duties of the wedding priest. It was very special. Damyanti and Samraj were there too. Rohini spent time with a lot of family and friends she hadn't connected with in many years. And, yes, Sonal also attended their wedding with her husband.

"*Didi, namaste.*" A familiar-looking woman came to her with a tray of tea and snacks as she sat on a couch, recovering from the long marriage ceremony the night before.

"*Namaste*, oh, thank you, tea is exactly what I was craving. And you must be Kamala. I've been seeing you everywhere but couldn't talk. I'm sorry. And please call me Rohini."

"You arrived here on the day of your wedding. There were a lot more important things for you to do than talking to me," she said, smiling and put down the tray on the coffee table.

"Oh, yes, I couldn't get here earlier but made it. It's always a good thing to be present at your own wedding, isn't it? Anyways, now I have the time to talk to you, tell me about yourself."

"Your mom was right. You really are nice to everyone. What can I say? My name is Kamala, and I do housework in lots of houses."

"And your family, children, what do they do?"

"Goodness, no one asks me these questions. Not the young people like you, anyway. They look through us like a mirror, as if we don't exist. I'm not prepared well to answer, but I will try."

"You shouldn't think that way. Not everyone is the same. Santosh, the housekeeper before you, lived with us, and we were like family."

"Yes, you are right. Your family is good that way, but let me tell you. It is rare, very rare."

"Anyways, so tell me. And for heaven's sake, sit down, lady. No, not on the floor, next to me in that chair."

"Thank you. Where should I start? I have three children, and an alcoholic husband who doesn't work and lives off my earnings."

Rohini smirked at the stereotypical situation in which Kamala's socioeconomic strata found itself across the country.

"And your husband must be beating you too."

Kamala nodded yes looking at the floor. Although her situation was quite common, there was something special about Kamala.

"*Didi*, ah, I mean Rohini, could you come to my house one day and meet with Chandu, my husband?"

"Of course; I would love to."

"And tell him what would happen to him if he continues like this. He knows you're a lawyer. That will make a difference."

"I'll do that, but you know what will make the real difference? When you tell him that with courage. Tell him you have had enough. You know what I'm saying?"

"Yes, but it's easier said than done. I have tried many times before. When can you come?"

"How about tomorrow afternoon?"

"Great, thank you very much. I can see why you're the favorite child. You're different from everyone I've met in your family. God bless you and may he give you health, wealth, and happiness."

"Believe me, it's not a big favor, just coming to your house and giving that silly man of yours a piece of my mind."

On their way to Kamala's house next day, she learned the rest of her story.

Kamala got married when she was only twelve, after her father's untimely death. Her mother couldn't raise five children as a single parent, and became dependent on her in-laws for sustenance.

"I was in school when destiny struck its hardest blow. I wanted to continue to study, but couldn't stop my uncles from marrying me off to a poor family. They said that was the best they could do for us."

"That's awful."

"At least my elder sister was lucky to have been married when father was alive. Her husband is a clerk in a rural bank. She is educated and working for herself. I'm happy for her but wish I was the older one. I know it's very selfish of me, but . . ."

"I know what you mean. No need to feel bad for thinking like a human."

"My marriage to Chandu is the worst thing to have happened to me, and no matter how hard I tried to get out of it, I failed. Since I've told him about my desire to get an education, he's made every attempt to keep me away from books. Now I just wish all my three children have the opportunity that I hadn't."

"Do they go to school?"

"Not all of them do. My eldest, Sukanya, lives with my sister and helps her run a small training center in her village. She basically does cooking and cleaning in return for training to be a quilt maker. Even though it wasn't my dream for her future, it's definitely better than Chandu's plans for marrying her off at thirteen."

"What about the other two?"

"My eleven-year-old son Mohan is in middle school, but unfortunately, school doesn't interest him as much as cricket does. He spends most of his time playing outside with his friends, most of them school dropouts but Anjali, my eight-year-old daughter, is bright, full of life, and a real charmer."

"I think I saw her during the wedding too. She's quite a social butterfly, and the sparkle in her eyes is unmistakable."

"Yes, you must have. I'm sure she would excel in school, but unfortunately, she has to hop along with me from one house to another. How can I leave her behind when I'm away all day? It is very unsafe for girls in our slum neighborhood. So I bring some books with me and ask people where I work to help teach her. It works, but not very well."

"Why is it so hard for them to help her learn?"

"Rohini, if we started educating our children, who would work in their homes to make sure their children are comfortable?" Kamala said as a matter of fact.

"Did my parents offer to help?"

"Yes, they did. I know your mom couldn't teach her, but she gave me money to buy the books. I am always indebted to her."

"Thank goodness. Ajit and I are planning to visit Ram Temple this evening. Would you and Anjali like to join us?"

"Are you sure you want to go with us?"

"Why not?"

"It has never happened before."

"That doesn't mean it can't happen now."

"Oh, I would love to. It's been years since I went to that temple."

"Alright then, be ready at six. We'll pick you up from your house."

Anjali looked happy to be in the temple and, for the first time, shared a conversation with the newlyweds. Rohini enjoyed answering all her questions.

"*Didi,* my mom said you're a lawyer. Do you wear the lawyer's gown, like in the movies?" "Aren't you scared of the bad guys?" "Do you live by yourself in Delhi?" "Are Ajit *Bhaiya* ("big brother") and you going to live in Mumbai?" "How big is it?" The barrage of questions kept them busy.

"Mom, can I go to Mumbai one day?" She turned around and looked at Kamala.

"Well, let's see. You need lots of money to travel, so when your sister starts earning, or your brother becomes a great cricket player, you could go."

What a hopeless situation, and an enduring hope!

"Anjali, I'll take you there one day. I don't know when, but I will."

"Oh, thank you, *Didi.* You're very kind. I know you always keep your promise. Your mom says that all the time."

They came home late at night, and dropped off Kamala and Anjali outside their little mud house in the slum, bordering the well-planned officers' housing.

"You know, Ajit, I often wonder about the symbiotic relationship between our plush, planned houses and their illegal mud huts. These people need work for survival, and we need their help to have a comfortable life. Indeed a simple case of supply and demand! No wonder our comfort is being threatened by those people's desire for educating their children. What if they succeeded in lifting their next generation out of poverty and dependence on the jobs we provide? You know, Mrs. Sharma was complaining about this craziness yesterday when she came to meet with me. She said that getting the cooking and cleaning help was becoming so expensive that she might have to stoop down to doing some of the work herself. Poor Mrs. Sharma! Imagine the tragedy."

"Would you like to mourn Mrs. Sharma's tragedy with a sweet *paan* (betel leaf stuffed with sweet spices)?"

Ajit had a knack for turning serious conversations into lighter, more entertaining ones, and she didn't mind.

"Absolutely, it calls for us to stoop down to that level of eating."

They loved *paan* from their best local *paan* corner they knew as little children.

"*Namaste*, Lakhan, how are you?"

"Ajit, and ah, you too, Rohini? What a pleasant surprise! You know I supplied *paan* at your wedding, but, sorry, I couldn't meet with you. Things were really crazy at that time."

"I could tell that the *paan* had to be from the one and only Classic Paan Center. The guests were raving about them too."

"Now you're embarrassing me with your kind words. Anyways, how could I help you today?"

"Two sweet *paans* for now and four to go, please." Ajit winked at Rohini and smiled.

"Hey, Lakhan, where is your son, Sameer? I remember seeing him at your shop most of the time with his books or playing with his friends," Rohini asked curiously.

"You just missed him. It was so crazy at the time of your wedding because we were busy settling him at boarding school. He left only two days ago. It was such a bittersweet thing to be able to send my boy to a good school after all those years of saving. His mother is devastated to see him go, and now I'm wondering if sending him away was such a good thing after all."

"Lakhan, I know what you're saying, but most importantly, your son will get a quality education and that can only be a good thing."

"Yes, that is true. I don't want him to sell *paan* like me, and only education will change his future. Do you know my son will be the first one in my family to go to college? You have no idea what that means for poor people like us."

They listened to him for a while and enjoyed the *paan* that never failed to impress. *Paan* is quite a messy thing to eat and dispose of. Once it's in your mouth (you eat the whole thing at once), you are unable to speak while chewing on it, and then you have to figure out whether you are going to swallow it or spit it in regular intervals like a professional. Lakhan was helping, since they were not obliged to speak while he ranted about the political, social, and religious situations in the country. When he slowed down, they tried to leave, but he kept going.

"I have seen both of you as little children, and am happy to see you together as husband and wife. You're really made for each other—educated, same caste, good looking, and perfect! I wish you both a blessed married life."

That's how people were wired to think—same caste. Rohini looked agitated and wanted to say something, but Ajit held her hand and smiled, as if to say that her reaction wasn't going to change the way Lakhan thought. She should just accept his blessings regardless of how he defined their union. After a lengthy speech, Lakhan finally let them go.

On their way home, Ajit and Rohini talked about their life in Mumbai together. She had to wrap up her work and life in Delhi, while he needed to upgrade from being a lazy bachelor to a responsible married man. That meant he needed to move out from his current one-room apartment in a shady part of Mumbai at Meera Road.

"I'm concerned about my frequent traveling for work, like I've said to you many times before," Ajit said.

"That doesn't bother me. I'm used to living by myself. Besides, that'll give me some space every now and then. At the moment, I'm more focused on what my house will look like. No, I'm just kidding!"

It was late when they came back home, and everyone was asleep. They went to sleep on the terrace under the stars for one more night, before leaving the next morning.

"It feels strange to be married into the family I used to visit for playdates. Come to think of it, we could be one of the very few couples to have this connection." Rohini whispered when they were about to enter Ajit's family home. He nodded in agreement and planted a kiss on her forehead.

It was special to have common childhood stories about their neighbors, schools, teachers, festivals, and shops. They had known their respective in-laws since childhood, but the fact of their changed relationship took some time to sink in.

Their common friends hailed their alliance as a "match made in heaven" for the same reasons.

"Why don't people understand that we married each other not because of what we are, but who we are for each other?" She got frustrated over comments along those sentiments.

"I'm glad *you* know why you married me. I don't care what others think."

The next morning, they said good-byes to their family and friends, all of whom had gathered since the morning to wish farewell to the newlyweds. They had a lot of common friends and distant relatives.

Rohini and Ajit started their life together in Mumbai in a one-room apartment. The material comfort was something to be desired, but they were happy together and made a great, fun-loving couple who became part of a large social circle. With friends from their respective offices and their neighborhood, they worked hard and played harder. Life was good. Or, so they thought.

He worked for an oil and gas company and had to travel intensively, so she tried to adapt to that reality and kept herself busy. New friends and the life of a single woman with the perks of marriage made up for the loss—only just.

As the time passed and the novelty of a financially secured, single life with friends faded, she started to notice Ajit's frequent travels. She kept a brave and loving attitude initially, but started resenting that he didn't read between the lines when she said she was fine with the arrangement.

She buried herself at work in a number of projects, and counted on a few good friends for emotional support when he was away. They became her lifeline and spared Ajit a lot of guilt when he left home for travel.

After being married for five years and achieving most of the standard milestones of owning an apartment, a nice car, and a decent bank balance, they were eager to have a family. When

Rohini missed her periods, they realized their life had changed forever. The new baby was an easy-going, fun-loving life that tickled and kicked playfully in the womb. It was a relatively easy pregnancy, and six months went by without any incidence. They wanted to take all precautions during the last three months, and given Ajit's frequent travels, Rohini went to spend that time with her parents in Bokaro. Since leaving her hometown for college, it was the first time she had come to stay with them for such a long time. Ajit visited each month, and they had the best time together. They liked their life in the mega city of Mumbai, but Bokaro's charm couldn't be replicated anywhere else. It was, and would always be, a special place for them and now for their first child too.

Somya, their baby girl, arrived a week before the expected due date in October 2000. Ajit could only spend a few days with the newborn before duty beckoned, and he had to travel overseas. Kamala and her daughters were her constant companions, and they seemed to enjoy that little addition to their daily life and work.

"Rohini, Anjali wants to play with the baby. Can she?" Kamala asked as soon as she opened the door for them.

"Speak of the devil! Mom and I were talking about you guys just now."

"Really? What about us? Only if you'd like to tell me, though." Kamala winked.

"Well, she was telling me that you had sent Anjali to work for a family but that didn't go very well. Mom didn't give me many details, but I understand she was unhappy there. Oh, silly me, I shouldn't have brought this up in front of her."

"No worries, she's fine for you to talk about it now, but it took her a long time to get back to normal after being rescued from that family. They broke my little daughter."

"I'm so sorry to hear that, but I don't want to make you relive the nightmare. Let's talk about something else. Anjali, Somya is sleeping but should be up soon. Would you like to eat something, like biscuits?"

Anjali nodded yes.

"Rohini, you're not doing anything like that, in fact, I would like to tell you about it a bit more. Anjali worked for that family for six months and endured six long months of hardship. I thought I was doing the right thing, but it turned out to be the worst decision of my life. My brother delivered milk to that family, so when they were looking for help with their kids, he thought Anjali would be a good choice. It didn't sound bad, looking after two little kids when their parents were away at work, but we were so wrong. They used her as a human machine for cleaning, cooking, and looking after children with no break in between. My poor daughter didn't get enough food or sleep. She became so weak that my brother had to sneak her out."

"She's a child herself. How was she expected to look after two children *and* manage a house?"

"Poor people don't have a choice other than to be strong. It's a matter of survival, plain and simple. I still dream for my children to get an education and have a decent job. My dire situation, however, has made me realistic over time, and I have lowered my already pitiful expectations for their future. It has now come down to making sure they're not starving. You must have noticed, I've started bringing Anjali to help me so I could work in more houses," Kamala said in a matter-of-fact manner.

"And what is your husband doing about that?"

"He's getting worse, if that was possible. He used to fight with me only when things went bad. Now he doesn't even need that excuse."

"You know you have the right to complain about him to the police. Have you told him you would do that if he continues? Do you want me to come to your house as I did before, and threaten him with that possibility?"

"That won't work. He knows I would never hurt my reputation in front of the neighbors and our family by calling the police."

"You know all that reputation bullshit really makes me angry. You are equally, if not more, responsible for your situation with him." Rohini started getting agitated.

"I know, but that's my fate. At this stage, I'm content with the mere existence of my marriage, children, and work. Oh, I can hear the baby, I'll go check on her." Kamala tried to end the conversation. The phone rang at the same time. Kamala went to the bedroom to check on Somya, and Rohini picked up the phone.

"Hello Mr. Kaushik, we're good. How are you? Are you back in town? That's what I thought. She just woke up. Anjali is playing with her. They get along so well. Yes, I know. Not looking forward to that really, even though I miss Mumbai. What? Bring Anjali with me? No way, her mom will never do that again. I'll tell you in person. No, a really bad experience. Yes, how would you feel about that? Once bitten, twice shy, I guess. No, there's no point talking to her. I'm telling you, Ajit . . ."

Kamala could hear the conversation, and was in front of Rohini as soon as the phone call was over.

"I heard what you were saying on the phone. I shouldn't have listened in, but when you mentioned Anjali, I started paying attention."

"Oh, I hope I didn't say anything I shouldn't have."

"No, no, please don't say that. In fact, I was going to say that I would be very happy for Anjali to go with you. She would want that too, I am sure. She loves the baby so much, and also repects you a lot." Kamala was beaming with joy.

"Really? After all that happened to her?" Rohini and her mom looked at each other in pleasant disbelief.

"If there's one place I could think of sending her, that would be yours. I know you and your family well enough to know Anjali will be treated fairly and will learn good things too. Your mom has told me about your passion for teaching. Anjali wouldn't take long to start reading and writing, given some help."

"I'm so thrilled, but also daunted by your confidence. Ajit and I would love to have her with us. I'm sure Somya would love that, too."

The Parental Side

"Hey, look, they're here," shouted Anjali's brother.

Rohini, Ajit, and Somya went to Anjali's house to pick her up for their trip to Mumbai. Everyone in Kamala's neighborhood seemed to be out in the street to see them. Soon, little children and curious adults started following them as they walked out of their car toward Kamala's house, a tiny mud structure in the far end of a series of small mud and straw houses. It had a small arched entrance that needed bending till the waist to enter inside and provided privacy from the public through a piece of cloth hung as a curtain. Rohini recognized the cloth as the bedsheet that had been in her room for many years. How could she forget the distinct navy blue hibiscus pattern?

"Have some *chai* and biscuits, *Didi*." Anjali's elder sister, who came back from her aunt's house to see her off, offered as soon as they entered the one-room hut.

The reception reminded Rohini of Samraj's daughter's wedding.

"Kamala, thank you for trusting me. I promise that Anjali will be happy with us," Rohini said, just before getting in the car with Anjali, opening her arms to hug her. Kamala nodded and smiled while wiping away tears from her eyes. The two classes seldom hug each other, so she hesitated before throwing herself in Rohini's arms and letting go of her emotions.

After the big procession of picking up Anjali from her home, they got into the car to ride home, and a sense of responsibility dawned on Rohini. She was now the custodian of someone else's child.

Anjali was happy in the car, playing with Somya. She didn't look heartbroken when leaving her family. Given her day-to-day life in her own home, it was quite possible that going to Mumbai to play with a baby might have seemed like a dream.

"You're such a natural with kids. Soon enough Somya will prefer your company." Rohini's confidence made her giggle.

During their journey by train to Mumbai, Rohini told Anjali about the city and their new house.

"Before I went to my parents' house for Somya's birth, we booked an apartment that is now ready for us to move into. It's my dream home, and I'm sure you'll like it too."

"*Didi*, I don't know what the houses there look like, but I'm sure it'll be great," Anjali said excitedly.

"If you ask me, frankly, I think Mumbai is a city of extremes that amazes and frustrates me at the same time. Wait till you see the contrast. Bokaro will seem like a haven of equality in comparison. Some people live in the most expensive houses in the world, and others die across the street for lack of food and shelter. Some get robbed of their dreams and become paupers, while others dream big and make it bigger." Rohini tried to read Anjali's expression, and wondered if she would embrace or dread Mumbai's paradox. She seemed curious to know more.

"I can never forget my first trip to Mumbai with Ajit, and how I nearly screamed during the plane landing. The airport is so close to a large slum that it seemed like our plane was going to land right on top of the houses and people. I could see children running around, and grown-ups doing their chores without even blinking when the plane made its landing, almost touching them. It seemed unreal, and I held my breath until I got out of the plane and inside the airport, still in shock. You should have seen Ajit's face. He was trying hard not to laugh at the situation. And that was only a brief introduction to what Mumbai stands for."

"That sounds crazy!"

"Oh, wait till you get in the local train. You'll be able to touch people's houses along the railway tracks. I tend to look inside those houses when I travel to and from work, and have been fascinated by how they've carved out a life in the middle of a railway system. They look completely unfazed by this frequent, fast, and dangerous interlude. The train also takes you closer to the riches and opulence of the city, and that is equally amazing. It took sometime before Mumbai got under my skin, and then I became one with it."

"And have you started loving it? What about the underworld gangs that we see in the movies? Aren't you scared of them?"

"Ha! Funny you should say that. I thought the same when I arrived, but I quickly figured out that unless you're extremely rich or rub them off the wrong way, they won't bother you. In fact, Mumbai is the safest place for women in this country. I traveled alone all the time for work, sometimes well after midnight, and never had any problems. It's an amazing city, to say the least, and I hope you get to know it as well as I have."

"I hope so too, *Didi*."

"I had a special affinity for the city, even before I arrived here five years ago. Ever since my shocking first landing, I looked for *Baba* in everything, and often wondered if part of my decision to marry Ajit was indeed affected by the fact that he lived in Mumbai. I remember talking with him just before the wedding. 'Hey, do you realize how amazing you are in linking your excitement for Mumbai with your grandfather's school there? Tell me honestly, was that the real reason behind you saying yes to marry me?' he asked jokingly."

"What did you say?"

"I said, well, that was not the *only* reason," Rohini blushed.

As she was recounting the story to Anjali, she finally admitted to herself that Mumbai not only enchanted her for its contrasts, but because she was spiritually connected to it through *Baba*.

Anjali didn't say much during the taxi ride from the train station, and looked a little lost. She was too busy gawking at the tall buildings, big shops, and lots of people. It was hard to tell if she looked excited or daunted since her expression changed frequently from one to the other.

"Look, the Kaushiks are here. Welcome home, guys!" their friends, who were waiting for a late-night celebration, shouted as soon as their taxi stopped outside the apartment complex.

"What a surprise! Thanks for coming along, everyone. Meet our little one, Somya." The proud father showed off his little bundle of joy.

"She's beautiful. She looks more like her dad, doesn't she?" one of them noted.

"She does, and good for her. Mom says that girls who look like their father are supposed to be lucky," Rohini said, holding Somya tightly.

"I hope so. Let's go inside and get the party started," Ajit added and smiled.

"And who else have you brought along from Bokaro? Is that a servant? Lucky you, dear," said Seema, one of Rohini's close friends, who always had something to say.

Anjali froze where she was, next to Ajit in the far corner of the kitchen. Ajit saw her looking sideways, so he held her hand and maneuvered the crowd to bring her in front of them.

"Sorry, I should have introduced Anjali to you earlier. She's here to play with Somya, and will stay with us for as long as she likes. We have also promised her mother that she will be reading and writing fluently in no time. She's an amazing girl. You'll find out soon."

"What a creative way to introduce your servant! I'm impressed! But I never thought you guys would bring a child to work for you, knowing your principles against that. What happened?" Seema looked at others for nods of approval. A few more nods flustered Rohini as she struggled to explain that she opposed child labor and having Anjali at home was not the same thing. Anjali retreated behind the curtain and wanted to disappear. *What a great introduction to life in Mumbai!*

Rohini tried explaining further, but they looked more interested in food and conversation about other things. Talking about a servant wasn't worthy of their precious time. They avoided any eye contact with Anjali throughout the night, who looked mortified and wasn't able to decide her next step, literally. She kept standing still behind the curtains, which weren't positioned well enough to cover her completely.

"Have you eaten anything?" Rohini lifted the curtain.

"It's OK, *Didi*. I'll eat when they go," Anjali whispered timidly.

"I apologize for everything. Please don't take it to heart. They're nice people, but they don't think before speaking. However, I think you should eat. They might be here a little longer than you can endure. Have something, freshen up, and sleep. Your bed is in the study."

"Here, Anjali! I've got your plate. Take it and go eat in your room if that makes it more comfortable," Ajit hollered behind Rohini.

"Thanks a lot Ajit, I'm so sorry about what happened. I had no idea they would show up unannounced and on top of . . ." Rohini tried to explain, but saw Seema coming her way. That was the last thing they wanted—another conversation with Seema in front of Anjali.

"Hey, Seema, I'll join you soon. Just hang in there." Rohini waved and started moving in her direction.

After a few hours, Rohini got tired and wanted the guests to leave. She sat with Somya in her lap, looked completely disengaged, and felt invalidated by her friends. She failed to convince them that Anjali was not brought for child labor, but for an opportunity to learn while she helped as a playmate for her daughter. They didn't seem to buy it at all, and that bothered her.

They eventually left during the early hours of the morning.

"I'm exhausted. Not sure our friends really made it better for me tonight." Rohini crashed in the bed, next to Ajit.

"Seems their less-than-approving vote for having Anjali in our house has given a blow to your moral high ground," Ajit commented sarcastically.

"What the hell does that mean? I'm not talking about their validation. I'm just too tired to go back to sleep, and it doesn't make me happy."

"Sure, but even if you are bothered, let me tell you, none of them think much of these things. They were giving you a hard time because of your previous objections to their housekeepers, and the condition they are generally kept in. I admire you for that, but I don't understand why you feel the need to explain and convert people to your way of thinking. If you're happy with Anjali's addition to our family, then be content with it."

"Ajit, you're unnecessarily making me think of something I'm not bothered with. Please let me sleep. Good night."

Sleep was far away from her that night, but staring at the ceiling to fix all her problems had no rival. When she eventually fell asleep, vivid dreams of Narayanpur and the glimpses of the summer vacations she spent there kept her tossing and turning.

The Heartless Side

"You know, it's been nearly six years since I came to Mumbai, and I'm yet to see *Baba's* school," she looked at Ajit and said as soon as she opened her eyes in the morning. He was lying next to her, reading a newspaper.

"Were you dreaming about that all night?" he chuckled, still looking at the paper.

"Goodness, how do you know?"

"I know everything. No, just kidding! Have you asked Raghu to take you there some day? You have his phone number, right?" he said while folding up the pages. He looked handsome in the mornings, she thought.

"I have, but I'm not sure why he never responds to my requests to take me there. I've also asked *Dadi* many times, and she tries to avoid talking about it, too. In fact, no one has even given me the address of the school, despite me asking for it on many occasions."

"That seems odd. Why wouldn't they want you to see it? Try once again, maybe later today. Let's talk to him."

"Just in case you've forgotten, you're leaving tonight for a month."

"Then you call him after I go, sweetheart. What's the big deal?"

"So you're saying that your absence shouldn't be a big deal for me when I'm juggling the duties of a parent, and looking after the mammoth interior design project in the house? How do you think I'll do all that, not to mention Anjali's education that I so confidently promised her mother? I haven't taught her a single thing to date, and she's been here eight months already. How am I supposed to feel about that?"

"That's a long wish list. Maybe take a few items off that, and just chill, my dear".

"You know I hate your 'be cool' preaching when you just sneak out of this mess and have a good time out there."

"I never have a good time anywhere without you."

"Whatever."

"Look, all I'm saying is you can't boil the ocean, so have your priorities in order. Your frustration over not being able to do everything is futile. Anjali hasn't been educated for most of her life. She could wait another few months. Please don't beat yourself up over that."

"Thanks a lot for that sage advice. I'm so glad I have your shoulders to lean on," Rohini raged with anger, ran into the bathroom, and locked it.

Ajit eventually managed to make peace before he left, but after that, things started to change between them.

In the beginning, Rohini resisted asking Anjali to help around the house. After all, she was there to play with Somya and learn. That plan didn't last very long, as she started taking an interest in doing more housework while Somya slept. Soon enough, Anjali stated cleaning, washing, and helping in the kitchen. Rohini also started meeting with friends and socializing often, as she became confident of Anjali's capabilities.

"I know you are trying your best to not treat that girl as a servant, but there is no denying the fact that that's who she is. I mean, come on, Rohini, we know she is the only help you've got. But, it freaked me out when I saw you guys having a meal with her at the same dining table last Sunday. Do you really expect me to eat at that table now? I haven't attained sainthood yet, and would think many of our friends share my sentiment. My dear, may I advise you do not get ahead of the society? It's a good thing to keep pace with the change, but to be so far ahead that everyone else is a distant second may not be a great idea," Seema, as usual, bombarded Rohini with her opinion as soon as she saw her at one of their common friends' house.

"What the hell? Rohini, are you guys out of your mind? I mean do you really eat with your servant, sitting at the same table?," one of the guests got excited.

"Do we really have to make such a big deal about that? Yes, Anjali has meals with us, so what? If that makes you uncomfortable, we won't serve you on that table. Happy?" Ajit said politely but firmly. Rohini looked at him with surprise.

"I'm sorry, Seema. I guess it isn't the right time for us to be here. We should go now." And they left soon after they had arrived. Not much was spoken between them on their way home, but they knew that peer pressure was building up, and Rohini wasn't coping well.

"Why do you think you have the moral authority to behave as badly as you feel like with my friends, and leave me with the consequences?" Rohini finally spoke, accusing him.

"And the consequence would be that Seema may not be willing to eat at our dining table?"

"Ajit, please don't make fun of everything. You have no idea what it's like to live in a society with its norms. All you do is bring in money, and I would like you to focus your energy on doing that. Leave the rest with me."

"I'm not having this circular argument with you anymore."

"It seems circular because you're at the center of it."

It didn't help that Ajit had to travel the next morning. Things changed a little more for the worse every time he left. Rohini pondered over the situation and decided to focus her energy on important things. First of which was Anjali's education.

"Anjali, is Somya ready yet? Let's go downstairs before the sunset." She called from the bedroom when it was time for Anjali to take Somya to the playground.

"You're coming to the playground, too?"

"Yes, I should get some fresh air, and I also wanted to talk to you about a few things."

"I'm nearly done changing Somya. I just need to get her milk bottles and will be with you in a few seconds, *Didi*."

"Ah, it feels so good to come here and walk in the park. Sometimes I forget we have such lovely surroundings so close to us," Rohini said as soon as they started walking around the playground in the middle of their apartment complex.

"So true, *Didi*. I really enjoy it every day, but it's even better when you are with us." Anjali smiled, held her hand, and started swinging it. She was very easy to please.

"I was thinking of making plans for your studies. I'll tell you more after walking a bit more. OK?" Rohini said, huffing.

Rohini was surprised by a number of women and children who greeted Anjali in the playground and looked at Rohini as if they were seeing her for the first time. She was yet to connect with her own neighborhood even after moving into the new house several months ago. She was also getting less fit, staying at home or socializing around.

"I am done. I'm really tired now. Should come down more often and get fit like you. Come, let's sit down on that bench and plan for your studies. You know a little bit already, don't you?" Somya had fallen asleep in the stroller.

"Yes, but not enough. I can count and read a little. Mrs. Singh told me I may have the first-grade level," Anjali said when they sat on the bench.

"Well, that's a great start, but looking at how much you have taken on in the house, it's going to be very difficult to manage. I think we should have Mangla back doing cleaning and washing from next week, and get your books and other things in the meantime. It'll be a lot of fun. I'm so excited! You know when I was in Bokaro, I used to run classes for Santosh, our housekeeper, and . . ." she stopped.

"And?" Anjali asked.

"No, just him, and sometimes my brothers. Yes, my brothers also sat in the class." A twinge of guilt ran through her for deliberately omitting her mom from the list of her students.

"You really like being a teacher, don't you, *Didi*? Many children don't get to learn because they never find people like you. My mother told me I was lucky to be with you and to be able to read and write one day. She has many dreams for me, and you came as an angel to help her. When I grow up, I would like to be a teacher. Maybe I could teach Somya her first letters," Anjali giggled with a sense of pride.

"You'll have to. Who else would?" Rohini smiled.

"There you are. I've been looking for you everywhere. I called you a few times on your landline that never seems to work, and your cell phone was out of reach." Seema was coming toward them, screaming as if there was an emergency.

"Is everything alright, dear? You look stressed." Before Rohini could complete the sentence, she was dragged away by her friend into a corner behind the bush.

"Rohini, you got to know this. I'm your friend, and I only want the best for you. You're a well-meaning person, but also an emotional fool when it comes to bringing anyone under your wings without thinking through the consequences. As your well-wisher, and I'm deeply concerned for you," Seema went on rambling and started to breathe heavily.

"Seema, calm down. Take a deep breath. What happened? And how am I an emotional fool? What's going on here? I've noticed you guys whispering a lot behind my back these days. I had been meaning to ask you if I needed to be aware of something you all know and I don't."

"I struggle to speak about these things with you since you are the savior of the poor, and we are somehow against it. And this girl you have brought from Bokaro, you can't trust her, Rohini. You just can't. I had also warned Radha, who, like you, blindly trusted her servant and didn't listen to me but came to her senses eventually. She and her family endured quite a painful experience, but better late than never, I say," Seema continued her mission to save her dear friend from a looming disaster.

"But what happened to her?" It didn't make sense to Rohini.

"*Didi*, I think Somya wants to go home." Anjali walked across the playground with the stroller where the two were talking.

"Oh, for God's sake, girl, can't you see we are talking? These people, I tell you." Seema shook her head in exasperation. She couldn't bear Anjali's presence.

"Look, she didn't come to listen in on our conversation, but to tell me that my daughter may be tired and ready to go home." Rohini stood up and started walking out of the playground toward the apartment building. Seema followed her. Anjali pushed Somya in her stroller and maintained a safe distance from both of them.

"Hey, girl, you mind making some *chai* for us? And give me the baby. I'll hold her. Never mind, I'll pick her up. Don't bother. Just go make some tea," Seema ordered, as soon as they reached the apartment, leaning in on the stroller and grabbing Somya out.

"Why are you snapping like that, sweetheart? What has Anjali done to make you so mad at her?" Rohini asked, teasing her friend.

"I'm not mad at her. I'm just doing what you should have done from the very beginning, showing that girl her right place. You are spoiling your servant her just like Radha did, and God forbid if you go through the same experience. Yes, you can say that I'm a little sensitive and emotional about it, but not without a reason. Only last night Radha called me in tears, and I went to see her straightaway. She was overcome with regret and paranoia, because of that thankless maid whom she treated like family, and trusted with her daughter. And what does she do? Robs her off and leaves her daughter intellectually disabled. You know, Mona can't speak even though she's four years old. Well, it turns out that the maid didn't look after her when Radha and her husband left for work. She would put her next to the television all day and keep herself busy on the phone, talking to friends and family. She also stole jewelry and clothes and sent them home systematically. Radha caught her red-handed yesterday when she came home early from work as she wasn't feeling well."

"*Didi, chai.*" Anjali brought in a pot of hot tea and snacks.

"Oh, yes, put it on the table and leave." Seema knew Anjali had heard a bit of their conversation and, after thinking for a second, said, "Well, no, you should listen to this too." She continued, "When Radha came inside, she saw a man sitting in her living room. As soon as he saw her, he started to panic and hurriedly locked up a suitcase. Radha insisted that he open it. She was shocked to see their watches, jewels, and antiques. You can only imagine what happened next." Seema looked pointedly at Anjali.

"Oh, how awful! I never thought Sheila would ever do such a thing. I really liked her." Rohini found a moment to speak when Seema paused to take breath.

"I know. That is why I've been warning you guys to think carefully before having a stay-at-home maid. I mean, if Sheila could do it, anyone could."

Anjali slowly began to pick up the cups from the coffee table and started walking toward the kitchen.

"Come on, Seema, don't be judgmental against every housekeeper. Just because one of them stole something, doesn't mean all of them will. Stealing, robbing, or lying is not confined to people helping you with housework. Everyone does that. You and I do that too in our own way, don't we? I am sad for Radha, but let's not get carried away and paint everyone with the same brush. That wouldn't be fair," Rohini tried to reason.

"My dear friend, you're in denial, aren't you? I am not saying only the maids steal or lie, but just look at this example. A maid's action over time affected a child so badly that she is unable to speak. Poor Radha, she paid big time for her trust in these people. I've learned my lesson and am never going to let any maid near my son. No one should risk their children's lives. It's just not worth it, my friend."

"*Didi*, can I start preparing for dinner? Ajit sir is coming home tonight." Anjali looked at Rohini, and she nodded yes.

When Seema left, Rohini told Anjali, "Anjali, I want you to know that none of what Seema said today affected me. OK? I trust you, and I know you'll never do anything wrong. You know what she's like, don't you?" As she tried to assure Anjali, Seema's words nagged at her, despite her efforts to push them away. Her friend had played the child-parent card very well.

"You do whatever needs to be done in the kitchen and bring Somya here. I'll give her a massage. It's been a while since I've done that, hasn't it? Seems like you have completely taken over this house, and even my child now."

Something had changed that day, and Anjali saw it.

Rohini was talking to her mother on the phone while Somya played on the floor. Anjali picked her up, put her in the stroller, and took her to the kitchen.

"*Didi*, I'm taking Somya inside. It's nice to see her play while I cook," she said and walked inside, and Rohini continued to speak on the phone. Neither of them made eye contact, seeking or giving approval.

Anjali was grinding spinach in the blender and got distracted by Somya when she started throwing up milk. As she tried to attend to her, she lost control of the blender and the spinach got splashed all over the countertop, and on Somya. She panicked and called Rohini.

"Oh my God, what have you done? Somya, baby, are you OK? Just stop the blender, for heaven's sake!" Rohini came in, screaming with rage, and gave a tight slap on Anjali's cheek. Then she took Somya out and went to the bathroom to clean her up.

"I'm sorry, *Didi*. I didn't do it on purpose." Anjali came in to the bathroom and pleaded. She burst into tears, and sat down on the floor with her head buried in her lap.

"Hey, who do you think is going to clean up the mess? Get off your butt and wipe it all up. If I see any stains on the wall, it won't be a good day for you." Anjali got up immediately, wiping away tears.

"You surely have become the stereotypical master of the house, dominating a girl barely twelve years old. You expect her to clean the house, cook for all of us, and look after a toddler while you have a good time with friends. It's amazing how far your expectations for her have grown," Ajit remarked one day when she had another meltdown, following a minor mistake of Anjali's.

"Would you mind keeping out of what I do, when you're away for weeks?"

That didn't leave him with much to continue the conversation.

They were in the living room, watching television.

"*Didi*, when are we going to buy my books?" Anjali appeared with Somya in her lap and asked her out of the blue.

"Have you hung out the washing yet?" Rohini asked, knowing full well that she didn't have the time to do it yet.

"I'll do it now, *Didi*. Sorry." She handed the baby over to Rohini and went to the laundry.

"If you don't have the time, I'll go shopping tonight and get some books for Anjali. Which ones should I get? English, Hindi, or both? Don't know how far you have taught her, so it will be great if you could help me pick them. Or better still, why don't we all go out and buy them?" Ajit tried to make it light.

"Are you crazy? I thought we were going to the movies. I have invited a few people too. Anjali was going to look after Somya, and I wanted to make sure the house is cleaned and everything is done before we go out. And just in case you're thinking I don't want to help her learn, let me remind you that I was the one who brought her here in the first place."

"I was just trying to help as I know you didn't get the time to buy her books yet. So if I offer to do that, what's wrong in it?" Ajit snapped.

Anjali could hear their argument from the balcony where she was hanging the clothes. "Ajit, I'm sick of all this. I just want my peace of mind. Would you like to stay at home and take over what I do and I'll go back to work? God knows that was so much easier. I don't know what I was thinking when I asked Kamala to send Anjali with me. Yes, I made the promise to educate her, and I still want to do that, but when do I have the time? If you could be a little more sympathetic, I would really appreciate it. Whenever you are around these days, you make me feel like I've broken my promise to Kamala, or I'm ill-treating Anjali and you are the messiah who shelters her. Why are you doing that to me? I'm providing her food and shelter, and, in return, she's looking after my baby and the house. How is that unfair? You have no idea what it's like to be ridiculed by friends who think I've got nothing else to do other than hanging out with a baby and an illiterate servant." She was fuming.

"I'm amazed at your priorities these days. You often told me how you felt for the housekeepers in your parents' house and picked up arguments in their defense," Ajit reminded her.

"Well, maybe my parents were always right, and I was too naive about how the world worked. I've started to see their perspective now. It's very simple. I provide her with a better life, and she returns the favor. The work is less tenuous, and the environment is better than her own home. I'm sure she thanks her stars every day. Now, are you coming with us for the movie, or should I tell them you would rather buy books for the housekeeper?" Rohini stood in front of him with both hands on her waist; she wasn't going to take no for an answer.

"Look, I really wanted to go to the mall and buy a few books. That's why I offered to get some for Anjali, too. Besides, Raghu's son called me this morning. He didn't tell me what he wanted to discuss about, but he sounded stressed, so I asked him to meet me at the mall," Ajit went overboard with the excuse.

"That's wonderful! I would enjoy my friends' company better without you anyways—free from the reminders of all those moral obligations I am failing to fulfill. Please go ahead with your plans. Meet with Manoj and send my regards to Raghu," she said sarcastically.

He knew how to deal with that too and said, "I will. We should also press upon them to take us to the school. I'll ask Manoj to organize that."

"Ajit, can we talk about that later? If your aim is to make me feel even guiltier by dragging in the school visit now, you aren't going to succeed. At this point in my life, I don't really care if I see that place or not. I don't have the time and energy to drown in my fantasy world of helping all kids get educated. I'd really appreciate if you didn't bring up that subject anymore." Rohini left the room and went to call her friends about the movie plan.

"Why do you have to interpret everything as my attempt to make you feel guilty for failing in your endeavors? Far from it, I was trying to shake you out of your unusual, selfish, and apathetic ways and show you the kind of person you really are."

"Whatever, I'm going to make a few phone calls. Please leave whenever you need to and don't bother me." She left angrily.

Rohini nursed Somya before leaving, while Anjali busied herself with tidying up the house, lest the boss unleash her fury again. Despite being the victim of harsh words and bad treatment from Rohini, she still maintained her energy and love of life.

What was making her such an angry person since Anjali came along? Did motherhood really exhaust her? Was she missing going to work and making a difference in other people's life? Did she really not want anything to do with Anjali's education, and preferred to keep her as the housekeeper? As Ajit mulled over those questions, he noticed the barrier of hierarchy between Anjali and Rohini was growing stronger each day.

"Anjali, eat dinner and don't wait for us to be home for cleaning up. I've kept Somya's milk in the fridge, and make sure her bottles are cleaned and sterilized. You could manage other things when she is asleep." Rohini gave rapid instructions.

"*Didi*," Anjali said hesitatingly.

"Ajit might get you some books tonight, but don't bother him as soon as he comes in. That's not the only thing he has to deal with in his life," she said without looking at her and pretended to furiously search for something in the dresser.

"It's not the books, *Didi*. I just wanted to say you look very pretty in this blue dress." Rohini felt sick in her stomach, and didn't know what to say.

"Well, lock the door carefully, and do not open it for anyone except us." This time she looked at Anjali. Her eyes were filled with tears while her face was still smiling. The guilt was about to overcome her, but she quickly dealt with it and closed the door behind her.

When Rohini came back home, it was late at night, and everyone was asleep. She saw Ajit lying on the couch and Somya sleeping on top of him. Anjali was sleeping in the study on a mattress. She looked at her and wanted to go back to being the person she really was, ask for her forgiveness, and hug her. She bent over, touched her forehead, and was taken aback; Anjali had a fever.

"Ajit, wake up. Anjali has a high temperature. Did she tell you when you came back? Wake up, will you?" She shook him nervously.

"Oh, what? Where? Really? Yes, she did tell me she wasn't feeling well and asked if she could go to sleep after doing the dishes. I didn't know she had a fever." He lifted Somya off his body and put her in the crib next to him.

"Let's check the temperature first, but we might need to take her to the doctor now. The fever is very high. I'll get the thermometer." Rohini was panicked.

Anjali woke up and looked at Rohini taking her temperature. She wasn't sure how to react, appeared a little confused, and closed her eyes again.

"Ajit, it's 102 F. I'll give her the medicine and see how it goes overnight."

"Yes, sounds good. I'll bring a cold pack as well. The temperature needs to be under control." Ajit said and started getting up.

"No, I'll do that. You stay here." Rohini put her hand on his shoulder and stood up.

Just when she left to get the medicine and cold pack, the phone rang, and Ajit answered. It was Seema checking on Rohini if she made it home all right after the party. He told her what was happening and asked her to call back later, but she insisted on speaking with Rohini, so he relented.

"Hello, you OK, dear? Oh, what a way to end your day after we had such a good time here! I'm so sorry for you. Hugs and kisses, sweetie!"

"Thanks, dear, it's not too bad, just the fever. She should be fine by the morning."

"Rohini, you certainly don't seem all right. Take it easy, my friend. Just get her checked by that homeopathic doctor in Plaza Center. He's good and really cheap. Let me know if you need help. I can send my driver to take her there if you like."

"Well, I was thinking of taking her to our family physician . . ." She tried to tell her the plan and looked at Ajit, who wanted her to finish the call and attend to Anjali. He whispered that Somya was waking up in the crib and he was going to settle her in.

"OK, I'll consider that and talk to you soon. Thanks a lot. Got to go, bye." She hung up.

"Anjali, drink something. Your mouth looks very dry." Ajit brought a glass of water for her.

"*Didi*, sir, please go to sleep. I'll be fine. Sorry about the inconvenience. I'm not sure why I got a fever." She looked at Rohini with fear.

"Don't worry about us, silly girl. Now drink some more water, and tomorrow we'll go to the doctor," Rohini said softly, stroking her forehead.

"Her fever has reduced, but I still think you should take her to the doctor today. She should rest and not stress about why she's sick. Poor thing, she is miserable, feeling guilty for being in the bed when she should be working." Ajit had woken up earlier, taken Anjali's temperature, given her toast and milk, and made his lunch. He gave a peck on Rohini's cheek, gave her a cup of tea, and was about to leave for work.

"Ajit, I'm sorry about the way I've been behaving lately. It's not like me to be so mean to people, let alone to a little girl." She put the cup down, followed him to the front door, and asked, "Do you really have to go now?"

"Sorry, sweetheart, I'd love to stay back if I could, but I promise, I'll be back home early. Let me know if you need anything. I'll send the driver, after he drops me off at the office." He hugged her before opening the door.

"No, that would be fine. Seema will send her driver, or I'll call a taxi. No worries at all." She fought back tears, and struggled to gather courage to face Anjali alone, given her own behavior lately.

"*Didi*, I'll do the dishes first if that's OK with you. Sorry, I was really tired last night. Even though I told Ajit sir I would go to bed after washing them, I couldn't. I'm feeling much better now, so no need to see the doctor," she spoke slowly, and the smile was still there to make Rohini feel guiltier than she expected.

"No, no, please don't rush. Go get freshened up first. I'll feed Somya, and when she sleeps, I'll get an appointment with the doctor." She felt good after uttering those words of kindness.

The phone rang.

"I'll get the phone. Could you bring the thermometer from the kitchen counter?" she asked Anjali.

"Hi Seema, how are you, dear? Did you not have a good night's sleep? You sound hung over," Rohini giggled.

"Oh, I am fine. You know me. I just got a little overboard with my drink. You tell me, how's your servant? I mean, Anjali. Are you still thinking of taking her to the doctor?"

"Not sure. She seems a lot better than yesterday, but I think I should if the fever is above 100. Anjali, come here. I'm still on the phone, but I can use the thermometer. Oh, it's 101, and there are rashes on your hands and your neck. My goodness, you have it all over your body!"

"What? She's got rashes? Rohini, quick, she should see the doctor. I'm sending my driver over to your place. Don't bother going with her. My driver can take her to the homeopathy practitioner and get something for her. It could be infectious, and probably dangerous for you or Somya to be around her," Seema continued.

Rohini paused for a moment and then said, "Seema, could you please do me a favor? If you could come over as well and look after

Somya while I take Anjali to the doctor, that'll be great. I shouldn't let her go by herself with the driver," she pleaded.

"As you wish, dear. I'll see you soon," Seema relented.

"Anjali, get ready quickly. We're going to the doctor. Seema will be here anytime now," Rohini said hurriedly.

The doorbell rang.

"Hey, come on in. Somya is still asleep, so basically, all you have to do is chill and watch TV or read—whatever you wish to do. Hopefully, we'll be back soon. Thanks once again for your help, dear."

"No worries at all. What're friends for? You know where Dr. Pandey's clinic is, right? If not, just ask my driver. We go there when my servants are unwell. Cheap and mostly effective."

Rohini asked the driver to take them to the family physician, a few blocks away from where Seema had recommended and saw a long waiting line. She paused on the curb, assessing her options.

"Madam, why don't we go to the homeopathy doctor? He's good. We just came past his clinic. It didn't seem full at all. Should we go there instead?" He started walking toward the car, and Anjali followed him. Rohini didn't say anything, and walked with them.

The homeopathy doctor was friendly and attended to Anjali well. He asked her and Rohini some questions and gave a few batches of sweet pills to be taken regularly for two weeks. When Rohini asked about the rashes, he said there could be many reasons, and they might go away as soon as the fever subsided. When she asked if it was contagious, he didn't seem convinced when he said, "It shouldn't be, but don't rule anything out."

They came home, and Seema opened the door.

"Thanks for everything, my friend, and I'm so sorry for all the mean things I've said to you." Rohini hugged her.

Anjali heard Somya cry and ran toward her room.

"Hey, please stay away from her until you are fully cured. Didn't you hear the doctor say you could be contagious?" Anjali froze. Seema, now validated, shot a triumphant glance at Anjali.

The visit to the doctor changed a lot more between Anjali and Rohini, for worse. Rohini didn't let Anjali go near Somya for the first few days and slowly began to keep her out of everything, until finally, she was confined to a mattress in the small study. When Ajit came back from his trip, he was appalled by the new arrangement.

"Why have you ostracized that poor girl? Is it necessary?" He looked inside the study, the door of which was half closed, and saw Anjali lying on the mattress and staring at the ceiling. He walked to the kitchen where Rohini was cooking.

"Well, you see, our baby is fragile and vulnerable to infection, and Anjali has developed rashes over her entire body that could be contagious. This is just my attempt at keeping my baby away from harm," Rohini said calmly.

"But did the doctor even tell you it's contagious? And if so, what could be done to cure that?"

"He couldn't confirm either way, and I would rather overprepare than get caught off guard," she said and started walking out with a disposable plate of food, heading to the study. She bent near the door and slid the plate across to Anjali.

"Here, your food. Get up and finish it. Don't bother coming all the way in to the kitchen. Just throw it in the bin outside the door. You heard me?" she directed coldly.

"You spoke with her as if she's an animal, and without any qualms about it." Ajit followed her.

"I'm only doing what's right for us."

"For heaven's sake, don't be so cruel to someone else's child to keep your own safe. I don't even recognize you anymore." He walked to the bedroom, took Somya out of the cot, and started playing with her. Her giggles soothed him.

"Ajit, would you like some *chai*?" Rohini asked from the kitchen.

"Yeah, sure, could you bring it in here? Also, some cookies, please," he said, believing any issue could be solved over a cup of tea and a few bites of a cookie.

Rohini appeared at the door with a tray full of what he was looking forward to. He also noticed that she had done her hair, and put lipstick on. It was working already.

"Oh, hey! Come over and join us on the mat." She wanted to resist but kept the tea and snack tray on the bedside table and sat next to him.

"You don't know how stressed I am about that girl's infection, and constantly trying to keep us safe. It's been a little exhausting. I just don't know what to do. I'm regretting bringing her over. I talked to *Dadi* yesterday, hoping for some support, but it didn't turn out that way. She went on and on about how *Baba* wouldn't have cared if Anjali was infectious. He would have kept her right in the middle of everything, and oh, by the way, she also reminded me about my failure in educating Anjali so far. I mean, give me a break. I'm not shrugging off my duty. I'm just trying to adjust to the new realities with a child, a sick helper, a traveling husband . . ." She paused and looked at Ajit, who smiled and held her in his arms.

"Have you told your parents about Anjali? I think her family should know that she is unwell. Don't you?"

"Yes, I called Mom, and she said I should wait a few more days to see if there was any progress before letting them know. She was concerned they might panic and ask Mom to send her back, but quite frankly, that would be a great thing. I just can't stand her in this house for another day."

"Really, are you that overwhelmed?"

"Yes, I am. I'll take her to the doctor again tomorrow, which will be a week since the treatment started, and if she isn't getting better, then I'll ask her father to come over and take her back." She was looking away while saying that.

"Don't you think it's our responsibility to make sure she is treated well and gets better before we hand her over to her parents? They won't be able to bear the expense of her treatment."

"I disagree with that, Ajit, since we haven't caused her infection. Even if you are right about our duties, I'm sorry, I do not have the patience or ability to do that alone. I'm quite happy for them to use the money we've deposited in her bank account for work, toward the treatment. I wouldn't ask for the remaining amount. Nor would I ask her to come back and stay with me. I've had enough of this emotional blackmail situation I find myself in, because of my promises," she said with a straight face and continued.

"If her father is unable to pick her up, Seema has offered to let her driver take Anjali back to Bokaro. She is one of the very few people who understands me and loves me for who I am and not what they would like me to be."

"That's very kind of her, but I think sending Anjali back home with a person she hardly knows wouldn't be the right thing to do. Let's wait for another week and see how she recovers. I've accumulated some leave that I could use, and take her back. I'll take a train to go and plane to return to save a couple of days. What do you think?"

"Are you serious? How have you suddenly found the time? Something you never have for us. In any case, I'm ready for anyone to help me get it done with. I'm so over with my romantic ideals of education for all. We all make our own destiny, and that's the only truth. I need to quit being a do-gooder to everyone. Honestly, I'm getting tired of all this. I need some sleep, which has been a while," she said and looked at him.

"You seem convinced about your thoughts, so as you wish." His curt remark made her furious, so she stood up and rushed to the guest room, locking it from inside.

Ajit opened the door of the study and caught Anjali by surprise; after all, no one went to see her since she had to move into that room. She was lying aimlessly, as was strictly mandated by Rohini. She wasn't allowed to come out of her room except for toilet breaks and a few rare visits to the balcony but only when Somya had fallen asleep in her cot.

"Anjali, I'm making tea for you. Freshen up and come to the dining room. Somya is also playing there."

"Sure," she said chirpily, and stood up immediately.

She was about to sit down at the dining table when Somya tried reaching out to her from Ajit's lap. He handed her over. She hesitated at first and then hugged her tightly. Tears rolled out of her eyes. It had been a long time since she snuggled with her best friend.

Somya was giggling, and Anjali was happy.

"Would you like to go out to the playground?"

"Yes!"

Ajit got up from his chair and started walking toward the bedroom when he saw Rohini standing near the door, looking shocked and angry.

"Do you have any idea what you're doing? That girl is contagious, and you gave her our daughter to play with? You stupid man . . ." She was loud and clearly deliberate in her words.

"Calm down, please. She is someone's daughter too. How would you feel if this was done to Somya?"

"Ah, wait a second. Now I get it. You fancy her. Am I correct? What have you been doing with her?" She turned around and slapped him on his cheek. He grabbed her hand and furiously threw her on the bed.

"How could you stoop so low? You aren't the girl I loved. I don't even know you anymore. What could I possibly do with a twelve-year-old child? Who does that kind of thing?" He was gasping for breath.

"My father did, to his own daughter. I don't need to look far to tell you who could do that. Any man could." She tried to get out of the bed, screaming.

"To hell with it! Enough is enough! I don't think that girl is safe here in this house with you. I'll take her back to her parents as soon as possible." He stormed out of the room. Anjali was standing outside, looking at him with fearful eyes. Somya was in the pram playing but eager for them to take her out.

"Ajit sir, I'm sorry. I never meant to hurt you and *Didi*," she started apologizing.

"Don't blame yourself for anything. You are not well, and we're not taking good care of you. I think you'll be better off with your parents. Rohini doesn't know what she is doing, and I apologize for what you have gone through. We'll leave for Bokaro as soon as I get the train tickets."

Rohini came out of the bedroom and went straight to the kitchen, so fast, she crashed into Anjali, who was standing between the bedroom and kitchen wall. They both froze for a few seconds before Anjali made way for her.

Rohini left home with Somya and went to Seema's house. Ajit tried calling her, but she hung up on him each time. He tried again.

"Rohini, I'm just calling to let you know Anjali and I are leaving for Bokaro tonight at 8:00 p.m. from Victoria Terminus, so you could come back home any time after that. I'll be back in a week, and we can talk this through," he said, calmly, but fast enough before she could hang up on him.

"Do what you want, but leave me alone. These two days have been bliss, thanks to Seema and her husband. I'm glad you are taking that disease back to her place. I don't need to talk anything through with you. Everything is clear. I don't know if I want to rush home immediately. Let me take my time and decide. Bye." She hung up and looked at her friend.

"Seema, I should go to the train station tonight to see them off. Ajit didn't ask me to come but told me the time and place for a reason. Don't you think?"

"My dear, why do you keep beating yourself up over that all the time? It's not your fault that your servant has a horrible, contagious disease. Grow up and have your priorities in order. I have seen how miserable you've been since you came here. You're wasting your time, feeling bad for that girl. Get over it. You have paid her family very well for the work, and as far as her education goes, it wasn't like she left school for you and you failed her."

"I didn't try hard enough. Excuse me, I should feed Somya and rest a little, I'm feeling exhausted." Rohini said and went in to her room with the baby.

"Dinner is almost ready. I'll serve it once you are done feeding her. Please don't sleep without eating. If you're sad because I asked you not to go to the train station, please don't be. Vinay will take you there, but there's no need to starve yourself over that." Seema got anxious about her friend's state of mind, and followed her into the room.

"Don't worry, I won't sleep without eating, and I'm definitely not sad for not being able to go to the train station. Even if did, it wouldn't solve anything."

"Precisely," Seema happily added and left the room.

When Somya slept, Rohini put her in the crib and tried to sleep. Her half-asleep brain took her to the events that had unfolded since she first met with Anjali. No explanation would take away the fact that she was unfair to her. *Why do people say mothers are the most selfless of all?* Motherhood made her do what she could never imagine doing to an innocent girl. That girl, meanwhile, took it in her stride with a smile.

She reached over for the phone and dialed.

"Hello, *Dadi*, how are you doing?"

"Is everything all right, Rohini? You don't sound yourself."

"Yes, everything is fine. I just called in to see how you were doing. No, I'm lying. Things aren't very good here. Ajit is on his way to Bokaro, taking Anjali back to her parents. I just blew it up, *Dadi*. Don't know how I could be so unfair to her and break my promise to help her get a better life. Ajit feels she is not safe living with me anymore. Well, I told him I've had enough of her . . . ."

"Did you try to stop him?"

"What's the point? As far as that girl is concerned, he's made up his mind based on a few bad incidents. Besides, he doesn't like my friend Seema who doesn't like Anjali a lot. So, you see where things were heading. I don't know why, but I suddenly got disenchanted by this idea of carrying the burden of educating everyone. I had good intentions when I asked Anjali's mother to send her with us, but things changed quickly. When she fell sick with mysterious rashes on her body, and I wasn't sure if that was contagious, I had no option but to keep her away from us and the baby."

"If you think you were right in doing so, that should be good enough. It seems to me that you were no longer driven by the desire to educate her, and she got a disease that could infect your child. I think many people in your position might have done the same thing. So is there anything I could help you with, dear?" *Dadi* asked lovingly.

"I feel bad about not being able to stop Ajit from taking her back to Bokaro. I didn't let him have a conversation, and I didn't even ask her how she was before they left. I'm sure she hates me, and rightly so, I'm no different from the family she worked for earlier. Oh, *Dadi*, how I wish I could turn back time."

"*Beta*, I know how you're feeling right now, and, of course, I know you never meant to hurt her. The stress of motherhood and responsibility of someone else's child must have been overwhelming. Isn't it weird how we as mothers do selfish things without even thinking about it? I know what you did is wrong in their eyes, and no amount of explanation will take it back. Just be patient. Everything will be all right with time, as they are better able to understand why you did what you did."

"I know it'll get better one day, but I want to fix it now. Anjali will tell everyone about it before she realizes why it happened." The fear of falling low in people's eyes stressed her out.

"It isn't going to turn around tomorrow, no matter how much you would like it to. Your *Baba* taught me that. As long as he was convinced it was the right thing to do, people's opinion never bothered him. I've told you a few stories about that too. Everyone makes mistakes. It's how well you recover from them, that is important. Being perfect is not always possible, but if you're willing to go through the process of improvement, you've made the real progress. You can do it way better than anyone. Trust me. You know you want to talk to Ajit. It doesn't matter who calls first. You'll get to speak with each other regardless. Isn't it?"

"You're right, it doesn't matter who calls first. I will. Love you, *Dadi*."

"I need to go to the temple now. Bye, dear. I'll talk to you soon."

As she put the phone down, it rang again, surprising her.

"Ajit?"

"No, this is Raghu."

"Oh, I'm sorry. How are you Raghu *Kaka*?"

"Not good, my dear. Things at school aren't going well, and I tried to keep you away from it all this while."

"Tell me, I'm sure I'll be able to handle that."

There was silence on the other side.

"Hello, *Kaka*! Hello, are you there?" She wondered if the phone was disconnected. Then she heard him sob but didn't know how to console him without knowing what was bothering him.

"*Kaka,* if it hurts you to tell me, you don't have to. Ajit is away, but I can pass on any message for him if you like."

"No, no that's not the case, I'm sorry for being such a weak soul. I just wasn't sure how to tell you that I've been ousted from the school. A staff member has taken over the place in the name of local employment. I'm considered an *outsider* despite working there for forty years, since I'm an immigrant from a poor state."

"Who let them make the decision to throw you out, after all that you've done for the school?"

"Long story, Rohini, but the land on which *Baba* built the school was granted without any proof of donation. It turned out to be unregistered, unclaimed land that belonged to the state. One day, Manoj happened to mention that in front of staff, and it seems this guy thought he could use that against us. Very soon after that, we had local political party members knocking on the door, asking us to vacate the school premises."

"When did all that happen? Does *Dadi* know?"

"Almost three years now. We thought we would manage to find some paperwork or at least ask the donor, but he died a long time ago. Trying to convince his children didn't work as they wanted the land back as well. I later found out that the staff colluded with them to get us out, and help them run a private engineering college in the building after closing down the school. And, yes, I told your *Dadi*. She was surprisingly calm to hear that, and warned me against getting into any legal mess over the land. She doesn't think we have any chance of winning this battle and dissuaded me against getting you involved in any way. I hope you understand my predicament. I didn't even want to tell Ajit, but he saw us visiting the lawyer's office one day, and told me he knew one of the sons of the donor. So I called today to find out if he had any update after his meeting with the donor's son last week." He stopped to take a deep breath.

"Yes, he told me he was going to meet with Manoj, but we didn't get a chance to talk about that. Well, he wouldn't have told me anything if I wasn't supposed to know." Rohini recalled Ajit sleeping on the couch with Somya when she came back home from the girls' night the week before.

"Yes, Manoj was supposed to be at the meeting, but he couldn't make it as he hurt his ankle that morning. Ajit told me he would call me back, so I was waiting, but now I think he must not have gotten any good news for us."

"*Kaka*, I'm a lawyer and have some good friends who'll take up this matter. You should have told me, despite what *Dadi* said. The case is certainly not an easy one to win, but the fact that the school has been there for a long time, providing service to underprivileged children should help."

"To tell you the truth, we've been struggling to make ends meet, so I'm not sure if we are able to sustain a legal battle. Our current funding source is drying up fast with the existing funders pulling out, and no new ones coming onboard. You should also know that a few years ago, one of our teachers was found guilty of sexually abusing a few children at school. We fired him immediately, but it had a massive impact on funding. No one wanted to be associated with the school after that, and who could blame them? That rogue staff went on lobbying in the name of outsiders doing the wrong thing in their state, and, not surprisingly, they have found many sympathizers. If you ask me, I'm too old for this."

"Oh my God, *Kaka*, is the school called *Damyanti Baal Vikaas*? I remember reading about the incident." It was surreal, she thought.

"Yes, and it has been in tatters since then. The issue of the land's ownership is simply the proverbial last straw on the camel's back. I don't have the energy or means to carry on. Hence, I've been seeking to get a peaceful solution to close the doors of the school and rehabilitate the students. Quite a few parents who could afford their children's education outside have already withdrawn, but I'm worried about the other less-fortunate ones. Those will end up working somewhere soon, and education will remain a distant dream for them."

Rohini's eyes swelled with tears at the sound of a broken man.

"*Kaka*, please let me help you. I understand why you aren't willing to fight to keep the school going, but please don't give up so easily. *Baba* would've wanted you to persevere. I'm sure we'll find a way. Even if you lose the legal battle for the land, you shouldn't lose the moral sanctity of the school you have so painstakingly managed and maintained. Bad incidents happen at other places too, but you have to emerge stronger out of that. Let's look at the pressing issue right now and work our way through the next ones. What did Ajit say about your thoughts of closing down the school?" She was curious to know.

"He said the same thing. You're both strong people and are advising me well, but I really don't want to get dragged into anymore hardship and shame."

"I won't force you to do anything you don't want to, but think about it again. I'll speak with Ajit and find out what happened in his meeting with the donor's son, and depending on the news, we'll work out the best way to proceed. Will that be all right? And, oh, does *Dadi* know about all that too, I mean the abuse case?" Rohini suddenly remembered to ask him.

"God forbid, my dear, that might kill her. No, I hope she never finds out."

"I hope so too. Let's address what's in front of us. I'll call you as soon as I speak with Ajit. Please take care of yourself, *Kaka*. Everything will be all right." Rohini hung up, and couldn't hold her tears any longer. The thought of many children ending up working and not learning, hurt her. As her thoughts shifted to the unfortunate girl who came to work for her with the dream of getting education, the irony of her empathy stared at her. She tried to close her eyes and sleep.

The phone rang in the morning, but her head felt heavy, and she struggled to wake up. She let the phone ring out and went to pick up Somya, who looked uncomfortable. She had a soiled diaper.

After cleaning her up, Rohini sat down in the rocking chair and started feeding her. She enjoyed the familiar relief from the milk letting down. Both were happy.

The phone rang again just when she was finishing the feeding.

"Hello, how are you?" she asked Ajit formally.

"I'm good, just missing you two," Ajit said, in his usual loving way. She missed him too, and wouldn't have told him so unless he said it first.

"I miss you too, and I wish I could undo what I've done to Anjali. I know it's not possible, but will she ever forgive me? Was she mad at me? Are her parents mad at me? What can I do to bring things back to normal?" A flood of tears poured from her eyes as she finished asking questions in quick succession.

"I don't think Anjali was ever mad at you, and she sends her regard for you and love for Somya. When we arrived, her parents were a little confused, but also happy to see her, especially Kamala, who seemed to have missed her a lot. They asked her about the sudden homecoming, and she told them since I was coming to Bokaro for some work, she asked if she could come home with me. Then Kamala noticed the rashes and almost immediately understood what might have happened. She asked if she was back forever, and Anjali didn't reply. I felt a bit uneasy around them. Kamala turned to me and said that they would return the remaining money that Anjali hadn't worked for, soon. I told them to use that toward her treatment, and left as quickly as I possibly could. Their friends and family had started to gather near her house, strangely similar to how it was when we had gone to fetch her." He stopped as there was no answer from the other end.

"Hello, Rohini, you there? Good, I thought we got disconnected. Hey, listen, don't let that bother you anymore. What has happened has happened, and we should learn from the experience and move on."

"I guess you're right. Thank you for understanding, Ajit. By the way, Raghu *Kaka* called yesterday. He was looking for you and wanted to know how your meeting with the donor's son went. I know why you didn't tell me anything about that matter, but, Ajit; I think I could have handled that."

"I have no doubt you would've handled it. But *Kaka* didn't want to hurt you when you had a lot going on, and your grandmother had strictly warned him against it. If he wanted to fight the legal battle to keep the school open, sooner or later you would have been dragged into it. When else should the in-house lawyer come to the rescue?" He tried to make the conversation lighter.

"So what happened at your meeting, and why didn't you let him know?" she demanded.

"Well, I didn't have much to report back on, nothing positive anyway. I foolishly thought I could use my friendship with him as leverage. I pleaded with him to consider the poor children who came to the school with their hopes and dreams for education. He wasn't moved at all, and went on to suggest that he could employ a few of them at his tea estate in Assam or his brother's diamond-cutting business in Surat. He said it would be wise for us to quietly exit, and avoid any fee that *Kaka* would have to pay if the matter went to court. I didn't know what to say."

"From what *Kaka* told me, he's not willing to fight any legal battles to keep the school open, but he's concerned about the kids. Now, you may argue that it's a bit hypocritical for me to talk about the children's education in jeopardy, given what I just did to a poor child."

"Listen, dear, you need to come out of that hole you're digging for yourself. Your regret won't make it any better, but learning from it, and improving will. If you want, I could ask Anjali's mother to send her back with me, but I don't think that's the solution. I say we should let her be with her family, get her treatment completed, and, when you and she are both ready to be back with each other, we can work on it. OK?"

"I understand, now could you please call *Kaka* and let him know what happened? Or do you want me to tell him instead?"

"I'll call him tonight. We should also invite him and his family over for dinner when I'm back, and discuss some options for him to get out of this mess."

"Sure, that sounds good. You're back in three days, on Monday, right? Should I invite them for dinner on Tuesday?"

"Yes, that'll be perfect. I miss you guys and can't wait to come home. Hey, listen I've got to go now. A few friends have come home to meet with me. Take care. Love you!" Ajit ended the conversation.

Somya was blissfully playing in the baby gym. The phone rang again, and Rohini was about to answer when she saw the caller ID. It was from Seema. She let it ring, made herself tea, and sat down with the newspaper. It was wonderful to be able to do simple things like that.

The Accepting Side

When the doorbell rang on Monday night, she ran to open the door, and there he was, with a rose in his hand and his signature big smile. They hugged, came inside the house, entwined, and went to the bedroom with Ajit stopping briefly to kiss Somya while she was asleep in the rocker next door.

That night Rohini and Ajit fell in love with each other again. They were in no hurry to wake up in the morning. It was bliss to be Somya's father and Rohini's husband, Ajit thought lovingly. All three of them were in one bed, on a lazy day. Rohini had asked the cleaning and dusting ladies to come in late so she could savor the moment.

It was a special day, and they wished nothing interrupted them—least of all a phone call.

The phone rang, and they looked at each other. Neither of them wanted to pick up, but when it rang the third time, Ajit got up and answered.

"Hello, Manoj, what? When? Oh my God! Hang in there, I'm coming over as soon as I can." Ajit panicked. He looked at her nervously, put the phone down, ran toward the closet, and started getting dressed.

"Let's get ready. We're going to the hospital. *Kaka* just had a massive heart attack. Poor Manoj, he didn't seem stable when he called."

Rohini froze, and didn't know how to react to the news. She just kept looking at him.

"Why are you staring at me like that? Get ready. I'll go downstairs, get the car out, and you bring Somya along. Or do you want me to take her with me and settle her in the car first? Rohini, come on, we don't have much time. Let's go," he begged.

"I'm ready. What else do I have to do? I'll get Somya." Rohini shook herself out of her state of mortification, and hurriedly started getting ready.

"The traffic in Mumbai is getting crazier. Sometimes I feel so happy I don't have to navigate this every day, to and from work. I'm better off commuting in a plane. Oh, for goodness sake, what is this?" He suddenly stopped at an intersection that was blocked due to some kind of protest going on. The hospital was half an hour away, and if they waited for the streets to be cleared again, it would be too late. He was losing patience and took a sharp U-turn to detour when he hit a motorcyclist who couldn't move in time. A big crowd gathered and started banging on the car, demanding him to get out. Rohini started to worry about what the crowd could do to him. To her surprise, Ajit came out of the car with caution, and managed the situation calmly. Fortunately, the motorcyclist was not critically injured; it was just a few bruises. He gave him some money for treatment, and also offered a ride to the hospital where they were heading. He explained why he was in such a hurry to detour. It worked, and the crowd dispersed and went to join in the protest. The motorcyclist counted the money Ajit gave him, looked at him in disbelief, smiled, and rode off.

Rohini wanted to say a lot of things, but decided to keep quiet and let Ajit regain his composure. He didn't seem to be in the mood to expand on what had happened. It was unlike him to be so impulsive and distracted while driving. The news about Raghu had shaken him, and all he wanted was to be in the hospital as soon as possible. It took them another forty minutes to maneuver the traffic.

She was lost in her thoughts when Ajit braked suddenly, stopping the car in the parking space. He got out immediately, gestured at her to get out of the vehicle, and started walking.

She carried Somya and rushed behind him to the emergency ward. He nervously asked about Raghu at the reception, and they were shown the way to the ICU. It seemed they had just arrived as well. The doctors were frantically attending to *Kaka*. Manoj looked shocked, and was robotically obeying the hospital staff's instructions.

Rohini and Ajit hesitated to enter the room, and glanced at each other.

"I think I should stay here with Somya, and you go help Manoj. I shouldn't have brought her with me. I'll feed her here in the waiting hall, and hope she falls asleep. Or better still, I should go back home. What do you think?" Just then, they heard a commotion inside, and ran in. Raghu breathed his last in front of them. It was unbelievable. Everything was over so quickly.

Manoj sat next to his father's lifeless body, and stared at the wall. The doctors wanted to speak with him, but he didn't respond.

Ajit went near him, put his hand on his shoulder, and said, "We are so sorry for your loss. It's difficult, but you need to be brave. Please let us know what we can do to help." Manoj didn't flinch or look at him, he just kept staring at the wall.

"Doctor, I'm a family member. Please tell me what we need to do." Ajit took over dealing with the body and the hospital management. After that, he helped Manoj with the funeral. It was to be held in Narayanpur, according to his father's wishes.

Ajit and Rohini went to Narayanpur for the funeral. If the number of people gathered was any indication, his life was being celebrated in a grand way. She met with her parents and *Dadi*, who managed the logistics and everything else. Her energy, even at old age, was unmatched.

After the funeral and the last rites were completed, the reality of the school children with nowhere else to go dawned upon them.

As they sat together, catching their breath after a long thirteen day ritual, *Dadi* came in, looking concerned.

"I'm heartbroken to see these children. Could something be done to help?" she asked, while settling into her intricately carved wooden chair.

They all looked at each other, but no one seemed to have an answer.

"You know how much I love them, but with the loss of both my father and my money, I'm not in any position to help. I hope you understand." Manoj made the first move and defended himself.

"Of course, I'm not expecting anything from you right now. You've given a lot to them already. I know they love you and will understand your situation."

"So what do you think?" She looked at her sons expectantly, who were unprepared for taking any responsibility.

"I guess if some of the older kids could be sent to families looking for domestic help, it wouldn't be a bad thing, would it?" Gopal said sheepishly.

"It wouldn't be a bad thing per se, but that's not the future they were dreaming of, Dad," Usha said hesitatingly, and got angry glances from him in return.

"I'll call my friends in Delhi who work in social services. They might help us." She looked straight into her father's eyes.

"Glad to see there's someone willing to support those that have been wronged. Now that I have you all here, there's something I need to tell you about," *Dadi* said, staring gravely at the anxious faces.

"A few months ago, Raghu called me to talk about the school. He was shattered, as he saw it as a personal failure and was deeply concerned about not being able to live up to *Baba's* expectations. Well, it's not just about his legacy." She paused when one of her employees came in with tea. She asked him to leave the tray at the coffee table, and gestured at him to leave.

"Some of you have asked me, and still wonder why I never went to Mumbai to live with my husband. Well, that's because he had his other family there." The sound of dropping jaws filled the air.

"What do you mean?" Rohini's mom jumped in with curiosity.

"He married one of the women who worked at the school as a cleaner. Her name is Neelam. She had to work after her husband died soon after marriage, and her in-laws shunned her. Her parents didn't want the liability of looking after her as they had given her in marriage, and thus, their parental duties were over. Being a helpless widow living in a slum, she was so vulnerable to predators that she would often come to work with bruises. Those were the result of her resistance to men lusting after her. After several of those incidents, *Baba* asked her to move into the school premises and be safe under his refuge.

She was young, attractive, and a widow, so life wasn't much different for her even in the confines of the school. *Baba* tried to shield her from the predators, and asked her to work with the kids and in the kitchen. Soon enough, rumors of her being his concubine started to make the rounds, and it became so ugly that one day she tried to kill herself. She slit her wrists and only survived because Raghu saw her writhing in pain in an empty storeroom when he went to check on the school supplies. It was a sheer coincidence that she didn't die that day. After her recovery, she wanted to go to Haridwar, and spend the rest of her life in an ashram. She was fatigued by the constant effort of warding off evil eyes and lewd rumors. *Baba* responded by asking her to marry him."

"Oh my God, how long have you known? And how the hell did none of us hear anything?" Gopal screamed. She looked at him sternly until he calmed down, and continued.

"When he came home that summer, he told me everything. Such was his honesty that I had to rise up from being just his wife, and embrace the new reality." It was hard to tell whether she gracefully accepted the truth, or was realistic about her complete lack of influence.

"Have you met her? What's she like?" Rohini's curiosity got the better of her, but the question was ignored.

"All I ever knew about her was that she cooked very well and looked after *Baba,* at least according to Raghu. She also knew her limitations and never attempted to come to Narayanpur, not even for his funeral. Once he brought me a beautiful shawl she knit, and that was the sole connection I had with my husband's other wife. Until now." She paused, perhaps to check the temperature in the room.

"And what a destiny! Just after three years of her second marriage, she lost her husband again, that too when he was here in Narayanpur. I don't wish widowhood even for my enemies, let alone the woman who shared this curse with me." She wiped away tears with the corner of her saree and looked around as everyone watched in silence.

"They also had a daughter, Swati, who was born after his death, but I didn't know about her for a long time. Raghu and his family looked after both of them."

"So you're telling us that we have a stepmother and a stepsister that we knew nothing about until today." Uday couldn't hold it in any longer.

"Yes, and if you're wondering where they are, both are here in this house. The school supervisor and the old lady with her are Swati and Neelam. I haven't formally acknowledged them, but I think I should. We all should."

"I'll bring them here." Manoj got up and came back with the ladies.

"*Namaste*," Swati said with folded hands. She was a petite woman in her forties with long curly hair and wore a cream and brown pastel *salwar kameez*. She didn't look married, as the *sindoor* or *bindi* or red bangles (symbols of Hindu marriage) weren't apparent. Neelam had gray curly hair and sharp features with clear, glowing skin, despite her age.

It was awkward for everyone.

"Why don't you come in?" Damyanti got up and offered them chairs as the others gawked at them.

"Mother, you didn't tell us where our stepmother is from, I mean, caste, family, anything," Gopal started the conversation, not in the right direction, of course.

"Oh, didn't I? Neelam is from a poor family in Madhya Pradesh. Her father was a blacksmith," she replied hurriedly.

"Wow, well done, Father! What an example! You really did practice what you preached." He clapped.

"So my stepmother and half sister are blacksmiths. Never in a million years did I imagine this day would come. Here I am, constantly striving to maintain the Brahmin purity and supremacy in this family, and my own father failed me." His voice was rising with each word he uttered.

"I was so cursed that even death didn't embrace me, and your father took pity on me and gave me refuge, whether rightly or wrongly. I know you wish it hadn't happened, but who could fight fate?" Neelam said politely but firmly.

"It isn't destiny. It's our father who played a cruel joke on all of us. He always did! He was too busy looking after the underprivileged to give his own family the privilege of his presence. My mother never knew what living like a family meant. He would just drop in, give her money and goodies from Mumbai, and leave as if that was what she waited for. Well, I'm glad a daughter of a blacksmith had that privilege." He sneered.

"Gopal, that's enough! I didn't invite them here so you could insult them. If I hadn't given birth to you, it would be hard for me to imagine that you're your father's son. A man who gave his whole life to the service of humanity would be ashamed of having such a narrow-minded son like you. I failed him, and clearly didn't raise you well," Damyanti shook with anger.

Gopal sat down on the bench and took a big sip of his now cold tea.

"Before we got into this drama, I wanted to talk about those children. What should be done? You probably knew what Gopal's view would be. Uday is more concerned with his image in society than anything else, so he will help only if it improves his prestige. Manoj has given up and is waiting for the school to close down. I don't expect my sons' wives to do anything against their husband's desires. And that leaves me with the four of you." She let her eyes linger on Neelam, Swati, Rohini, and Usha and let the rest glare at her for calling them out so bluntly and publicly.

The juxtaposition of both carrying the burden of guilt for shattering Anjali's dream, and being counted among the sympathizers of the unfortunate children was awkward to the point of being painful.

"*Maasi* ('Mom's sister'), we need help with eight out of the forty children, but I'm particularly concerned about the five girls whose parents are never going to bring them home. They are a liability to them, and the school was simply a means to dump them somewhere, guilt free. We could bring the girls home to live with us, but right now, even we don't know where to go after the place is closed. I'm looking for a job everywhere, but the scandal at school isn't helping. So far, I haven't come across anyone willing to give me a chance, but I'll keep trying. Something will definitely come up," Swati said.

"When do you need a place to live?" asked Usha, just when Rohini tried to say something.

"Very soon. They're going to take possession of the school building in three months, and we have to vacate before then. I also went to talk to the donor's son, and asked if I could work at the college that he was replacing the school with. He said he could try, if I was willing to sleep with him. I don't think I'm that desperate yet. If I had the means, I'd have taken up the legal battle for our school. God willing, one day that may happen. I know it won't be just a matter of having the money to fight the battle. There are many vicious forces to deal with as well. The donor's son is connected to the politicians, who are connected with the underworld. It'll be a great challenge to take up when the time comes," Swati said confidently, even with the hurdles she outlined.

Rohini felt the presence of courage. She had read about it in books and heard stories of *Baba,* but to be face-to-face and side by side with a person who was willing to risk everything she had was overwhelming—so much so that she didn't dare offer help. What could she give to someone so willing to take up challenges for others, when her own ideals and big dreams about helping meant nothing?

She was in awe of Swati who was comfortable being a single woman from a questionable union in a prejudiced society. She couldn't fathom being so confident in that situation.

The story of *Baba's* second family in Mumbai, and their presence in the house spread like wildfire in the village.

"*Kaki* ('Aunt'), what am I hearing? Tell me it's not true that a low-caste woman and her daughter are here with you, and that they are none other than our respected *Baba's* concubine and their illegitimate daughter." A seemingly concerned distant relative came to see Damyanti who was sitting on the patio, massaging Rohini's hair with coconut oil.

"Speak with some dignity, Ganesh, will you? Neelam is *Baba's* wife, my co-sister. I don't feel obliged to answer your questions, or explain anything."

"Of course you don't want to tell us what happened, but that's fine. We all know about it, thanks to the clean-hearted Gopal. He's a minority who hasn't been blinded by the charisma of his father, who still seems to have cast his spell on this village. Marrying a low-caste young girl and leaving his own family here was by no means a noble thing for a *holy man* to do. I'm ashamed of being related to him in any way. Unless you kick that woman and her shameless daughter out of here, I don't see how we could keep our relationship with you. I hear the daughter is still unmarried. Well, like mother, like daughter, I say. She must be looking for a cashed-up upper-caste man too." Damyanti stood up and gave him a tight slap, taking him completely off guard.

"You'll regret it, *Kaki*. You'll regret it very soon. I'll see who comes to Raghu's funeral feast tomorrow after I spread the word around. We should've outcasted you a long time ago, but better late than never." Ganesh left, infuriated.

"Wow, Grandma, that was something. I didn't know you could do that," Rohini said, both excited and nervous.

"I couldn't take it anymore, even though I know he is going to do exactly what he said. We have to be prepared for very few people coming to the feast tomorrow. We may have to go door to door, talking to people and personally inviting them. There will be some questions asked, and a lot of people may choose not to attend, but at least we would've tried. Can you help me, dear?" She looked at her, begging with her eyes.

"Of course, *Dadi*, just tell me which doors to knock, and I'll get started. I'm sure others in the family would be willing to join me as well."

"Given the caste politics of Narayanpur, we should have the kids from the school, and Swati, go to the lower-caste side of the village, while you and Manoj do the upper side. Usha is good at it. She'll help you, too."

That afternoon, on a warm sunny day, five groups were ready to invite everyone in Narayanpur. Raghu's funeral feast marked the last stage of his life's celebration, so Damyanti hoped to have all his well-wishers gather and remember him together.

Swati was ready to go to the low-caste side of the village with Samraj's grandson, Bhola. Damyanti knew, that despite being too obvious and perhaps a little biased, sending Swati and Bhola would definitely make things easier.

Rohini and Usha went to the few prominent, rigid Brahmin families who were most likely not going to attend, if they had already heard from Ganesh.

Manoj took a few children with him to some of the houses that were likely to attend, but an invite would seal the deal. The two sons kept out of it. Gopal was vehemently opposed to anything his mother was trying to achieve, and Uday didn't want to be involved for the fear of upsetting his brother, and a lot of people in Narayanpur.

At a traditional upper-caste funeral feast, the lower castes were not allowed to eat during the first round of serving. They had to wait for their turn and eat outside the house. *Baba* wanted that changed, to make sure everyone sat together and ate at the same time. He was obviously too far ahead of his time, and those that arranged for his funeral didn't believe in his ideals, and maintained the tradition. Sadly, that feast was marked by the very discrimination he fought against all his life. At the time, Damyanti was consumed with grief, and was not in a position to protest.

Over the years after his death, India had begun to witness significant political and social movements to change the status quo of the upper caste's dominance. By virtue of special recognition for the scheduled castes and tribes, some extremely underprivileged citizens were granted job reservations since the Constitution of India was drafted, after its independence in 1947. This was further extended and broadened to include the Other Backward Castes in the 1990s. Though things were starting to change on paper as required by the new laws, at the social level, both upper and lower castes struggled to adjust to the new reality. People from the lower caste were presented with better opportunities for college admissions and jobs through reservations. The upper-caste children, competing for those college admissions and jobs, felt that they were paying for the previous generations' wrongdoings, and that their future prospects were being unfairly limited. Like most changes, it was coming faster to the cities compared to the villages. Narayanpur's were turning even slower because 80 percent of its residents were upper-caste. Raghu's funeral could be a rare opportunity for bridging the social gap, if they chose to take it.

Next day, as was suspected, many people didn't come to the feast. The attendance from the exclusive class was dismal, but, it was heartening to see that some chose to join in—those that cared enough to see past the caste and class barriers. As *Baba* had wished, everyone sat and ate together. It had been a worthwhile effort.

Rohini and Ajit came back to Mumbai and life resumed.

"No matter whom we lose, getting back to where life was before the loss seems to come naturally to us. But depending on what was lost, it changes us forever," Rohini said, staring at the ceiling in her bedroom.

"Someone's being philosophical today," Ajit remarked.

"No, really, I can't take my mind off what's happening with the school, the discovery of my new family, and the children who are unwanted, even by their parents."

"That *is* sad. I know what you're saying. Your aunt and stepgranny are quite tough, though. They'll work it out, I'm sure of it."

"Yes, but they need help. I'm such a coward, Ajit. When *Dadi* was asking around, wondering what to do, I kept quiet, fearing someone might look to me for help. I live in the same city where my *Baba's* legacy is going to the dogs, but never looked into Swati Auntie's eyes lest she asked for any favors. I don't know what happened to the 'eager to help' Rohini. Anjali's episode has shattered me, I think. You know, when I asked Mom about Anjali, she refused to talk about that matter. When I prodded her again, she told me Kamala no longer worked for her and has apparently gone around in her community, convincing people not to work for them either. Mom said they were rebelling against what they see— Brahmins exploiting the lower caste—and it all happened because of the way I treated her daughter. According to them, Anjali fell sick because of the way she languished in our house."

"Really? But that's not true."

"It doesn't matter. They all believe it as their truth. Mom and Dad are disappointed in me for humiliating them in the community. In fact, Dad's ashamed of being my father, and not surprisingly, Mom thinks he's right in his disappointment." Rohini broke down.

"Are you supporting your mom's premise, too? That would be unnecessarily harsh. You did surprise me by your behavior with Anjali, but I realize there was so much going on at that time. To make it worse, you also had a friend making you feel like you were stooping low in the social game by being too close to a housekeeper. Who knows, you may have been experiencing postnatal depression. I know you haven't taken Anjali's departure lightly, but don't let that weaken you. Rather, think about how we could turn that around and fix it."

"You can't fix things like that, not when your own parents are consumed with guilt and shame because of a promise you couldn't keep. It also didn't help that Anjali's father called them names for what I did to his daughter. He said that we were slave drivers, and worked his daughter so much that her body burst into rashes. He went on to threaten Dad with a strong retaliation from the lower caste."

"Bullshit, I don't understand why it's being treated as a caste issue. What's wrong is wrong, no matter who did to whom."

"Regardless, I'm very sorry for making them go through this humiliation. Trust me, I never intended it that way."

"Look, even *you* know that Anjali's father is a rogue drunkard, and I'm sure he's not concerned about his daughter's health any more than he is about the money he was going to get from her employment."

"Yes, but how many people are going to believe your version of the truth? I feel as if I'm being sentenced in the court of public opinion. Dad is considering moving to another neighborhood, as he can no longer bear the shame. I'm not sure how to feel about that. A high-caste Brahmin cornered by a low-caste father of a housekeeper might be a great example of the social change many have been hoping for. But it doesn't feel right."

"Well, as long we define each other as upper or lower, no matter who is exploiting whom, it won't be a *great* social change by any standard. I think it goes back to the debate about equality and fairness. Just because, now the lower caste and the upper caste can threaten each other equally, doesn't mean it's fair as well."

"You're right. Look outside, that nimbus cloud is going to burst open and pour down soon, and I'm craving *chai* and *samosa*. Are you?"

The Foreign Side

"Boy, do I have news for you?" Ajit called from Jakarta at 4:00 a.m. As usual, he woke her up way too early. But it seemed that the news couldn't wait any longer.

"Hello, yes, Ajit, what happened?" A big yawn came from Rohini who was still half-asleep, and struggling to make sense of what he was saying.

"Oh, I'm sorry about waking you up sweetheart, but I need to ask you before making an important decision that affects both of us."

"You always wake me up. What is it now?"

"I've got an offer to work in Perth, Australia," he said abruptly.

"When? How long till you're back? I was planning Somya's first birthday party, and it would be nice if you were here."

"I'm not talking about a short work trip. You know, the company's India business isn't roaring at the moment, and the only choice they have is to either relocate or let go of the employees. Which one would we rather choose? Besides, I thought you always wanted to go to Australia, didn't you?" this woke her up for sure.

"So you're telling me you have an offer to relocate to Australia, with us, forever?"

"Yes, pretty much not the forever part, but you may have the choice to opt for that later. The company usually sponsors a permanent visa."

"So if I say yes, I'll have to resign from work that I started only six months ago and leave my brothers, who recently moved to be closer to me. Your news also comes at a time when I finally started being happy again."

"Oh, look, I'm not trying to coerce you to leave all that and move to another country. As long as you are OK with the prospect of me losing my job because we wouldn't like to live in Australia, I'm happy to decline the offer."

"Why do you always make it seem like I'm opposed to what you want? I didn't say it would hurt to explore what life could be there. I was just articulating what our decision to move would mean."

"Great, so should I say yes to my boss now?"

"Tell me you haven't said yes to him already."

"You know me better than I know myself. Love you, honey. Go back to sleep now, and I'll see you on Friday."

"Of course I'm going to sleep now, thanks to your great news, husband, and why not? We MUST shake up the status quo every now and then."

"I absolutely agree. That's exactly why I love you so much. Also, I wanted to tell you that I need to leave for Perth in two weeks and you guys will come over as soon as your visa is stamped, which shouldn't take too long."

"Ajit, you bastard! I hate you! You had it all planned out, and made it sound like you were seeking my permission?"

"Tell me if you're happy or not."

"Yes, but . . ."

"Happy or not?"

Despite attempting to be at ease with the news, she was far from it. She certainly wanted to travel around the world, and Australia was high on the list, but leaving everything behind to live there was not something she had planned to do.

"Oh, my goodness, Ajit, why are you forcing me to be happy about news that hasn't even sunk in yet, and that doesn't need my approval anyways?"

"Because it's important for me to know that you're happy with this development. Things moved quite rapidly here. My boss had to make quick decisions about who to send where and on what terms. If I didn't keep up with his pace, I might have ended up with no job or, worse, a non-family transfer with a commuting schedule. You know how tired we both are of that. So when he offered me the Australian option, it seemed like the best available. Just think about it. I may not have to travel so much, which means we might have a normal life after all."

"I get that, but we don't have enough time for such a big move. You're leaving next week, and I have to uproot in a month. It's making me nervous, Ajit," she admitted.

"It'll be just fine. Keep faith, and you're more capable of managing it than you think. I know it's not easy, but I definitely think it would be worth it."

The phone conversation ended, and the transfer process began in full swing.

The next thirty days brought mixed emotions, as her mind was scattered in all directions, preparing for the new life in a foreign land. She often got lost in thoughts, reliving her childhood, school and college years, meeting with Ajit, and, of course, Anjali. Fixing the wrong was still unfinished business. While she got busy making calls to family and friends, letting them know about their move, she never stopped wondering if she could get in touch with Anjali and tell her how sorry she was for what happened. Her memories of Mumbai were forever intertwined with Anjali's brief and unfortunate stay.

Since she made their decision to move to Perth known to her friends and relatives, a lot of people came in to say good-byes and give their wishes. Compared to happy messages from a few, the number of concerns, suggestions, and cautions that came her way started to make her anxious about the move, and question her preparedness. In her heart, she knew it was going to be fine, except that she would miss her brothers and little sister. They had grown up into fine young people and were very supportive of her. Most of all, she wasn't prepared for her parent's view on the move.

Renu cherished her children's education, their careers, and ability to make informed decisions—all those privileges she didn't enjoy. She never wanted the shadow of her illiteracy and powerlessness to affect them, and Rohini's decision to quit her job disappointed her.

"Rohini, the twins gave us your Perth news. Is it true that this time Ajit's move is a permanent one, and you're going with him too? Are you sure about that decision? I mean, you just started working again, and I know how much you wanted and needed to do that. I believe a job is the most empowering gift you give to yourself and you should never compromise on that. My lack of skill to work in the corporate world is the only reason your father doesn't treat me as an equal," she counseled her daughter on the phone.

"Mom, I understand your views about women choosing to stay at home despite a good education and the ability to work. I admire your relentless effort to make sure we got the best education, so we don't have to go through what you did. I know you're worried that I quit my job, but it's not like I'm never going to work again. Did you know Ajit has been offered an office-based job, and he won't be traveling much? After five years of living the single married life, I'm so happy with the prospect of seeing him come home every day, that my career doesn't weigh high in comparison."

"Sure, *Beta,* you're educated and obviously are able make your own decisions, so do what you think is the best for you. Now your dad would also like to speak with you." She handed over the phone to him.

"I think your mother is right. We had a dream for our children that each would become someone of status in the society, and we have worked bloody hard for that. But you've always done things your own way, despite us trying to guide you in the right direction. For example, you know I wasn't a big fan of you attending law school, as I knew you were capable of doing medicine. I still don't understand why you wasted three years completing a science major, if you had to become a goddamn lawyer. I finally accepted that you chose to be a lawyer. If you worked hard to became a successful one, I would have accepted it, but now I hear you quit your job and are moving to Australia. What are you going to do there?"

"Dad, like I just said to Mom, this is not the end of my career, but it's definitely the start of a normal family life, so I would like to enjoy that first. My qualifications and capabilities are not going away by moving to Australia. In fact, a break would be good for us."

"Now, just so you know, I'm not saying this to benefit myself. I know you'll achieve anything you set your heart on, but it hurts me to see you wasting your education. Your mom and I are also a little concerned about you moving so far from us because it will be difficult to see Somya grow up as easily. But what can we say other than wishing you the best in life? We hope your decision is indeed a good one."

"Sure, Dad, I understand and I would love to talk more, but Somya needs to go to the playground. Only a few more weeks left for her to play with her friends. And please don't worry about not seeing her. We'll visit frequently, and you can come over and stay with us, too. It's not that far away. Oh, someone else is waiting on the other phone line. OK, then, bye. Say bye to Mom too. I'll call you soon."

"Rohini, dear, I heard you are moving to Australia. I'm a little sad about seeing you go so far, but I hear Ajit won't have to travel much. How fantastic! I'm too old to travel, so I'll miss my chance to see some koalas and kangaroos, but send me photos." Damyanti went off before Rohini could say hello, and she filled the conversation with excitement radiating from her voice.

"Thanks, *Dadi,* yes, I'm happy with the move. Did you know that little children don't work as servants in Australian houses? And you can't bring your housekeepers to work for you either. They also don't have *Brahmins* or *Shudras,* or any castes for that matter—just people. Can you imagine how great it'd be to live in such a place? Oh, I'd always dreamed of such a world, and now I get the chance to live in one. What do you think of that?" For the first time since

Ajit called with the news, Rohini had come alive with excitement and dreams about her new life, and giggled like a little girl.

"I'm so happy for you, my dear. It's been such a long time since I've heard your bubbly voice. Hey, you know, something has been bothering me for a long time, and I don't know how to get this monster off my chest." She treaded the "should I tell you about this or not" territory for a few seconds and continued, "I refused to live in Mumbai with *Baba* despite his pleas and regretted that. Each time he came home, I wanted to say 'Take me with you. I'm ready now' but never did. Despite doing that a few times, I kept thinking he would ask me once more and I would grab that moment with both hands. After seven years of long-distance marital life held together by his three-times-a-year homecomings, I was ready to have a real one. I was all prepared to plead with him to take us to Mumbai when he came home that summer. I dressed up in a beautiful *Rajasthani chunri* saree. Remember the one you saw in my box and wanted to wrap around you, and I said, 'Take anyone, but not that'? You didn't even ask me why and took the yellow one and left. Oh, I wanted to tell you everything, my child, but I guess you were too young to relate to it then. I looked ridiculous in that bright pink saree and loaded with jewelry, but that was my state of mind. I was insane in that moment of longing to see him and finally tell him what I had been putting off. He came home, and, as usual, the villagers thronged to see him as soon as he arrived. He cherished that moment of being the messiah when people told him their miseries and he promised to heal them. The lower castes had their turn after the upper-caste meetings were over, and, for reasons beyond me, he never tried to change that tradition. He probably wanted to be the great one for both, separately. Who knows? Anyways, I kept waiting for him, and when he finally came in to see me, he was too tired and hungry to notice how I looked or what I wanted to say. He picked up Gopal on his way in, and started playing with him.

"'Going to a wedding or something?' He looked at me and smiled.

"'No, why?' I was blushing with embarrassment. He let go of Gopal, came closer to me, and said he wanted to talk to me about something important. My heart skipped a beat. I wondered if he was going to ask me to come with him." Her voice started to croak, and she slowed down as Rohini's heart paced up.

"And what did he tell you?"

"He told me about Neelam and his marriage to her a month before."

No more words needed to be said or understood. She knew why *Dadi* was so happy that she was going to Australia with Ajit.

"So he had a home now, and I didn't need to be there."

"What did you say?"

"What could I say? I just pretended to understand him and the circumstances in which the only way to save a widow from the barbarians was to marry her. I said he had my love and support, and, in fact, I couldn't be more proud of him. That was the biggest lie. I was jealous and shaking with rage, but didn't know what else to say. What he had done wasn't going to change if I didn't agree."

"Then?"

"He said he was proud of me for being a strong woman and always knew I would understand and accept his decision. But you know what? I've thought about it many times. Tell me how hard it would've been for him to feel obliged to marry a beautiful young girl when his own wife was living away. I'm not a fool to believe it was purely to save her from evil eyes." Rohini felt submerged in the big waves of *Dadi's* emotion and was desperate to be rescued. Could *Baba* do such a thing out of lust? Even if that was true, she didn't want to know. He could do no wrong. Never.

"I know you're glad that I'm going to Australia with Ajit, but please don't project the past on *Baba* like that. You know he wouldn't have done it purely out of lust. You've always told me how much he loved you." That was her best attempt to come out of the waves without drowning.

"My dear, I know he could do no wrong in your eyes, but he was a human, a man, to be precise. If his own wife refused to live with him, his options for satiating his basic needs must have been limited. I don't blame him for what he did, but I'm not being naive to think that marrying Neelam was yet another act of kindness on his part. You're free to make your own judgment about it, *Beta*, but let me at least have the freedom to see it for what it was. Anyways, I don't want to poison you against him. I just wanted to say how happy I am that you are doing the right thing and going with your husband to start a new life. I wish I had done that too."

"I know, but you surprised the hell out of me and shook the very foundation of my belief in *Baba* through this version of the truth you chose to show me today. I'm not averse to knowing the truth, but it's not easy, and seldom sweet. You see, it's easier for me to idolize him for marrying a widow and saving her from the ugly fate that surely awaited her. But *Dadi*, even if he did it out of lust, how many Brahmin men were willing to marry a low-caste widow in those days? He could have kept her with him, without the sanctity of marriage."

"Yes, that may be true, and I have only myself to blame, but I was so heartbroken and angry with him that I had to get even. And what I did was unthinkable. Have you ever noticed how similar your father and Samraj look?"

The truth came crashing down on Rohini like a lightning bolt. *What is she talking about? Is my father not Baba's son? And am I not his granddaughter?*

"When he came home after six months and I was already four months pregnant, he didn't need to do any calculations to come to the obvious conclusion. But you know what made me feel really small? He didn't say a word or ask any questions, but just shared his happiness for the pregnancy and looked forward to his second child. Your father was always his own son, despite the truth looking right in his face. I didn't need to tell anyone who the father was, as Uday grew up to look more and more like Samraj."

It made sense now. Her father did look like Samraj, and she wondered if *Dadi* had truly risen above the caste barrier, or if a lower caste's blood in her son's veins made her empathetic toward them. Knowing her father's identity sent shivers down her spine, and the shock and disbelief were weighing heavily on her. *Baba* had been her ever-present friend, philosopher, and guide. *Why did she choose to become the medium for her to connect with him? Why did she imbibe her with all great things he had done and her undying love for him?* Rohini liked that version of truth better.

"Hello, are you there, *Beta*? Hello? Please talk to me. Don't make me feel any worse than I do already. I know it's hard on you to grapple with the truth, but I had to tell you before my end. I owe you that."

"No, I don't think I had to know any of that, and you didn't owe me anything. You were hell-bent on sabotaging my whole life's premise that you and *Baba* were superhumans, and ahead of your generation. I revered you both as the bridge builders we needed for this fractured, caste-ridden society of ours. How do I come to terms with the fact that it wasn't really from the goodness of your hearts, but your selfish needs, that made you appear to have transcended those barriers? I'd rather die ignorantly under the beautiful cushion of lies, than live to suffer this burden of truth. I hope you've found some peace after getting it off your chest, but what about me? Whom do I turn to? Thank you so much for the wonderful bon voyage. I wish you well, but may I ask that you don't introduce me to anymore ghosts from the past?" Her rage knew no bounds.

"*Beta*, I really am sorry. Believe me, that wasn't my intention at all. You're right, I should have taken the truth to my funeral pyre. Please forgive me, if you can." The finality in her words scared Rohini, but she was distraught, and in no mood to reconcile. After an awkward silence, the phone got disconnected from the other end. That was the last time she heard her grandmother's voice.

Was anything else left to be confronted with, before she left this country?

Since Anjali went back to Bokaro, Rohini barely maintained her friendship with Seema. When she came to see her before her departure to Australia, their conversation started formally and included standard questions about how she was feeling, if she knew enough about living in Australia, would she ever come back to India. But, surely enough, Seema couldn't help herself, "My dear, you may love the postcards from Australia, but make no mistake. There will be no servants cooking, cleaning, driving, or looking after your daughter. You'll become a second-class citizen, and a servant in your own house. I believe we have quite a royal life here, that shouldn't be traded for anything." Rohini sat in front of Seema, looking uninterested, and let her deliver some more words of wisdom before opening the door and gesturing her to leave.

As their new life started in Australia, the Kaushik family enjoyed the novelty of the place, the people, the community, and the scenery. Most of all, they cherished spending more time together. Rohini and Ajit loved being there for each other, and seeing Somya blossom into a beautiful Daddy's girl.

Rohini made many friends, and was pleased with her new community that looked after each other, regardless of what they were and where they came from. People weren't defined by their caste or class, and she appreciated not being bound by those barriers anymore. Contrary to the concerns from her well-wishers in India, she found it refreshing that people didn't have underage housekeepers and didn't boast of having servants. Household services were provided by professionals, not underprivileged, helpless children sent by their parents for sustenance. Being born and raised in a society of contrast between people based on gender, education, money, class, and caste, the relative equality mesmerized her.

The new life in Australia seemed to have turned out the way she had imagined. After the initial phase of getting to know how things worked and people interacted, she quickly found that people were the same all over the world, with similar ambitions and desires, with only minor nuances that set them apart.

Within the next couple of years, they became parents again. Sohum, their son, brought loads of happiness to them, and Somya was besotted by her little brother. Rohini also started working where she came across a different, albeit subtle, supremacy war based on cultural backgrounds. It didn't bother her much, since what she saw here was nothing compared to where she came from.

She was determined to keep her beliefs and disbeliefs suspended, and knew she could do it; after all, she had seen much worse.

She missed her friends and family, and was aware of the tyranny of distance, but she had no complaints about life in Perth. She related to, and was at ease with, her new world order.

She was also keenly aware of not being in touch with *Dadi* since their phone call before leaving India. She thought about her a lot, but didn't call. It wasn't meant to be.

"Ajit, wake up! *Dadi* is no more. She is gone." Sweat broke out on her forehead, and she wasn't able to breathe.

Rohini was at her funeral filled with guilt and sorrow and trying once again to understand the matriarch who didn't have a fairytale life. She was strong for those who knew her, and fragile for those who knew her really well. She counted herself and Samraj among the latter. He was there, busy as usual, working around the house and saying not much. Even at such an old age, his sense of duty for *Dadi* and her house was unwavering. She couldn't keep her eyes off him as the funeral went on. *Was that the end of his secret? Did he know about his son? Did he and Dadi have a lasting relationship or was it just one or a few nights of sleeping together? Did he know she slept with him to get even with Baba, or did he take it as a deeper love?* Her eyes wandered every time she saw her father near Samraj. *Did he not see what was so obvious?* But then again, she hadn't noticed anything either, until *Dadi* told her. *Did Samraj's family suspect anything? Wasn't it hard for him to go on with his life, as if nothing happened?* She always remembered seeing him in the house. He must have been there with his son, without being able to be his father. She was dying to know the answer to all the questions her baffled mind and overwhelmed heart asked. *Why did Dadi leave behind such a monstrous truth? Will I break the promise I didn't make, if someone else knew what I know?*

Hundreds of people from Narayanpur and neighboring villages gathered for the funeral. Neelam and Swati were conspicuous with their absence. Understandably so. Rohini wondered how they and the five girls, whom they had to seek refuge for, were. She hadn't been in touch with them since Raghu's funeral, and they never made any attempt to contact her either.

"Rohini, is that you? Remember me?" a heavy voice from behind shook her.

"Ah, I'm not sure, but I know I have seen you before. Hang on. You're Santosh, right? I mean Santosh *Bhaiya*. Wow, I never thought I'd see you here. Mom told me you went to the Middle East, Doha, I think. Isn't that right?" Face-to-face with her former housekeeper brought back many memories of his services to her family. He had grown leaner and sported a big mustache.

"Yes, that's correct. I'm so glad you remember me. You're still the same, big-hearted girl who respects everyone, and never makes anyone feel small. A lot of masters and their children don't even want to recognize their housekeeper, let alone know their whereabouts. God bless you. Yes, I did go to Doha to try my luck at making some money, but when I went there, the only job I could get was shepherding sheep. Ha! Can you believe it? It didn't work out. The locals would steal the sheep, and the master used to cut my wages and whip me twenty times for each missing sheep. It was the same life in a different country. Here, at least I was with my family. I have three children, two girls and a boy, and I made sure all of them went to school. My daughter is married now, and is a schoolteacher in her village. She even tried to send me money from her salary, but I'm not a sinner to take my daughter's money. I've given her away in marriage, so she belongs to her in-laws, not me anymore. My younger daughter is in high school and my son is in middle school. They make my life worth living. I'm not a rich man, but definitely a happy one. Your grandma was a noble woman. She always made sure that my children didn't miss school because of the lack of money, and made it available whenever I needed it. God bless her soul. You get the kindness from her. I heard you live in Australia now. What is it like there? I hear they have summer in December and winter in June. First, I didn't believe it, but my son told me why that is so. He's very smart and makes my heart grow bigger each time I think about his future. My children laugh when I tell them about you trying to teach me and your mom."

He smiled, as his eyes filled with tears. Rohini wanted to get a few words in while he was talking, but no such luck.

"I am so happy to hear that, *Bhaiya*. I always remember you whenever I think of my childhood in Bokaro. Both you and Mom were terrible students, but I didn't mind. I knew you were busy serving the rest of us as well, and I was probably demanding too much." She chuckled.

"So do you have a housekeeper in Australia and are you teaching him or her as well, huh? I'm sure they are better students than we were."

"No, we do not have a housekeeper there. We use a cleaning service agency once every week, and even that is too expensive. Children don't work in houses over there. Isn't that great?"

"Oh, really, that's too bad. What about the poor low-caste people? How do they get any money for sustenance if their children aren't working?"

"There are no castes there. And poor people get help from the government."

"What do you mean there are no castes? How do you know who is who? It must be very confusing then. Or only the high caste gets to live there?"

"Like I said, there are no high or low castes. Everyone is a person, and that's all. They have some other social issues but not the caste one, thankfully."

"Oh, poor Rohini, I feel sorry for you. No housekeeper and no caste. What a strange place to live in!"

"No, *Bhaiya*, it's a good thing. Can't you see? Little children go to school, and don't work in houses, and no one is placed high or low because of where they were born. I'm happy to be known as who I am, not what I am. Please don't feel sorry for me." She wished he could see what she meant.

"Oh, OK then, if you say so. I'm still not able to understand how people live without knowing their caste. How else would they identify themselves and each other? But I'll take your word for it. It might be good for Australia. Let me know if you need a housekeeper, I'm happy to come with you. I'll try not to be a bad student this time." He was joking, of course.

"You had bad students? I never knew you were a teacher in your previous life." Ajit came from behind and put his hands around her waist.

"Oh, Ajit, meet him. He is Santosh *Bhaiya*. You might remember he worked at our house in Bokaro."

"Of course, I do. Hello, how are you? I met your son just now. He's brilliant with general knowledge, and easily beats me. I'm sure you are very proud of him." Good social skills came naturally to Ajit, and his mere presence made people feel at ease. Santosh looked very content with the compliment, and bowed in *Namaste*.

"Hey, I wanted to speak with you whenever you have time. Somya and Sohum are playing with your parents. Do you want to go to the orchard?" He winked at her.

"OK, Rohini, Ajit *Sir*, time to leave. I'll see you at the feast on Thursday. *Dadi* was the mother of our village, especially for the downtrodden like me. God bless her soul. I'm sure she died happily and went to heaven. Our prayers won't go in vain."

"So, shall we go now?" He held her hand and pulled her toward the back door, which was the only way for them to leave the house without being seen by the elders.

They walked out swiftly, and ran like teenagers into the orchard. It was a nice breezy spring afternoon, and the mango trees were loaded with strongly scented flowers.

"I would love to come here in summer and eat up all the mangoes. Would you come with me?"

"This summer? You're not serious, are you? That's like, three months away."

"Why not? I can get some time off, and I'm sure your work will be only too happy to get rid of you for a few more weeks."

"Tell me honestly, what is this? Did we come here to frolic around in the orchard, while people are mourning, and working hard to put up the feast that's barely two days away?"

"Absolutely! I'm sure no one even noticed we're missing. Besides, we're celebrating your grandmother's life by frolicking in her orchard. It makes sense to me."

Rohini sat down under a tree, and Ajit settled his head in her lap and looked up at her.

"Tell me one thing. I've been watching people in and out of the house all the time, and it's interesting to see the dynamics here, compared to Raghu *Kaka*'s funeral with all that high-caste-low-caste drama. But I noticed Samraj has been acting a little odd. I saw him hiding in the back of the house this morning, crying his heart out, and then coming inside, as if nothing happened. I can see why a man wouldn't want everyone to see him cry, but this is something else." Ajit's forehead wrinkled with strain, his brain struggling and looking for the missing puzzle piece.

"Well, he and his generations prior have worked for our family, and *Dadi*'s death marks the end of it. We'll probably have to lock up the house, unless his family agrees to look after it as caretakers. I think he's entitled to mourn the loss of his employer and so much more." She almost bit her lip when those words came out of her mouth.

"I see, I see. It makes sense. But is it just me or, oh, God, I can't believe I'm saying this. Please forgive me for my craziness, but somehow your father looks a lot like him." Her heart sank.

An hour later, when Rohini finished explaining everything, they were looking at each other, dazed. *What do they do with that knowledge? What should have happened then? What should happen now?* They didn't know any better. Ajit wished he hadn't started that conversation. It was three hours since they came in to the orchard, and someone *did* notice their absence. Renu was coming toward them with Sohum, who was wailing his heart out.

"Ajit, please don't tell this to anyone. Swear by me. Please! Mom is coming this way. Try to look normal. You look like you've been stung by a scorpion."

"Well, I have been."

"Please, let's talk about this more tonight, not now. OK?"

"Sure." Ajit agreed.

"Sohum, my darling, what's the matter? I just came out here to have a walk with Daddy." She reached out for him, but he pulled away and hugged his grandmother.

"Let's go, *Beta*. Dinner is ready. I think Sohum needs some time with you, away from the crowd. He seems a little overwhelmed, and Ajit, you've been running around a lot for the last few days. I think you should rest before the long journey back to Australia. If you wish to eat in your room, I'll have it sent there." Serving food was the best way Renu thought of helping anyone. After all, that was the only language she knew. Rohini loved her mother, and her cooking, but wished they could talk about other things too.

"Mom, it's OK. We'll eat with everyone else. I'll feed Sohum whenever he's ready. Let's go now."

After dinner, Rohini went to put Sohum in bed. Somya was busy with her aunties and uncles on the terrace, flying kites. Ajit was still in the patio with her father and uncle, planning for the feast.

When Sohum slept, she came out of the room and started pacing on the veranda, waiting for Ajit. Suddenly, she saw something move in *Dadi's* room across the veranda. She ran outside toward the patio.

"Ajit, come here, please, quickly!"

"What happened? Is everything all right?" Her uncle turned around.

"Oh, Uncle, I just wanted to check something with Ajit. I need him just for a little while. He'll be back soon." Her father and uncle looked at him and nodded. Seeing him wait for their approval didn't necessarily make her very happy, but she admired her husband for his regard for elders.

"Who's in there?" They knocked at the slightly ajar door of *Dadi's* room. No one replied, so after waiting a few seconds, they knocked again softly. Just when Rohini started thinking she might have hallucinated, they heard a sob and pushed the door open.

"*Kaka*? What're you doing here?" Rohini switched the light on, and closed the door from inside.

Samraj was sitting on the floor, holding one of *Dadi's* shawls and crying. It was a pitiful sight.

"Nothing, *Beta*, I came here to check everything was OK. I thought someone should, you know." He was frightened.

"No worries *Kaka*, I understand. *Dadi* told me everything. I know. We both know." Rohini put her hand on his, and he burst into tears.

"She has gone, and I don't know why I am still alive," Samraj spoke coherently now.

"Did you love each other?" Ajit blurted out.

"She only ever loved one person, and judging her by a few nights of indiscretion wouldn't be fair." Samraj's voice grew stronger.

"Did you?"

He looked up and said nothing.

"Did she know you loved her?"

"I never told her, and she didn't need to know. She was already broken by her husband's second marriage, and that was torturous enough, I guess."

"Didn't you feel awkward, seeing Dad grow up in front of you as someone else's child?" Rohini wanted to know.

"There were only two people who knew that fact, until now. And only one person ever thought of Uday as my son, and that's me. Your grandmother never let me have that right, and, if it was possible, she would have it erased from my memory altogether. After all, she was the master of the house, and I was a mere servant. She never let anyone cross that boundary, unless she wanted to." Samraj punctuated every sentence with a sob.

"Oh, that's awful. Poor Dad! The father he thought was his, died before he got to know him, and the father he didn't know about was always near him." She was choking on her words.

"I was content with seeing him grow up around me. It wasn't easy, but there was no other way. Even though your grandmother always made me keenly aware of my position, she used to tell me about her plans for his future. She was obsessed about his education, wanted him to be a scholar like *Baba*, and secretly wished he took over the school in Mumbai one day. She braved all the adversities a widow in our society faces, to make sure her children had the best of everything. I helped her all along, since looking after *Baba's* widow and her children was my supreme duty, regardless of what happened. Given what he had done for this village, my service was nothing in return. While she was alive, I felt like I was still helping in some way, but now that she is gone, I'm lost. Oh, how I got carried away! I should go now. It isn't right for me to be here any longer." Samraj stood up and was about to open the door when it was pushed from outside.

"You all think no one knows who fathered Uday?" Rohini's uncle was standing near the door when they opened it.

"Uncle?"

"Even a blind man could tell. The best-kept secret of Narayanpur! Ha! Everyone knows why we're the messiahs of the lower caste. Let's not pretend otherwise. Or, do you want me to make it any clearer?" Rohini felt bad for Samraj, who was petrified and kept his gaze to the floor. Gopal's bitter words were a regular occurrence for Samraj, but he might not have felt it pierce his heart like that before. He looked at Rohini and Ajit, walked out, and they never saw him again. Ever.

An ethereal combination of grief and celebration was palpable at *Dadi's* funeral feast, with at least six hundred people united by love and respect for the deceased. It was a union never seen in that fractious village before. The poor and low-caste finally exercised their right to grieve for their beloved matriarch, at the same time, in the same place, as the rich and high caste. Not surprisingly, Samraj and his family were absent. Gopal was seen walking around, looking smug.

The Awakened Side

L ife resumed in Australia, as Rohini got immersed in her job and family. Things were working well, and according to plan. There were moments when she felt like she deserted India, and disappointed a lot of people who needed her assistance, but she didn't know how she could have made any difference. Whenever she thought about Anjali and Swati, she couldn't help but self-reflect, and that bothered her.

"Ajit, don't you think we ought to go back to India, and be helpful in some meaningful way? I mean, is this how we had intended to be—away from our roots, turning a blind eye to many who could use our help?" she asked him frequently. But that had become more of a habit than anything else. He barely had to nod before she would move on to other things, like who should join them for the next Broadway show in town.

Over time, she also started bearing enormous guilt on behalf of all Indians for the social evils of the country, and yet, nothing much happened beyond the feeling. The relationship between her birth country, fellow members of the diaspora, and non-Indians started becoming more complex. She got flustered when anyone prodded her about India's poverty, gender bias, corruption, or anything even slightly negative, and took it personally. She found herself defending India's caste system based on its history and going overboard, describing how it was distorted to suit a few, who declared themselves superior to others over time.

On the other hand, she frequently argued with fellow Indians who glorified their heydays in India, especially reminiscing having servants at their beck and call.

"Rohini, why did you have to embarrass Tulika in front of everyone? She was just being nostalgic about her life in India, and you jumped in, asking how old and well-paid her *servants* were, and whether they had ever gotten a chance for education. I couldn't believe it. Of all people, you should be the last one exerting any sort of moral superiority over that matter. Let's not throw rocks at other people's houses. We are in a big glass one ourselves. And all thanks to you, I must add. I'm sorry, but I'm not having anymore of your farcical and pretentious arguments." Ajit rarely lost his cool, but when he did, Rohini listened. They were in the car, driving back home from a social evening. Thankfully, the children were at home with the babysitter.

"Why do you keep harping about India's social evils when all you have is your dream? How about showing some mettle and actually doing it? There are many poor, underprivileged children here and everywhere in the world, who could do with some help. But if your definition of poor and underprivileged is country-specific, I'm happy to quit my job and go back to India. Would that fulfill your dreams of charity?"

Silence.

"Look at me and tell me. Will that help?"

She was looking outside the window. He was right, and she didn't have the answer. "Rohini, the clothes you are wearing, the diamond you're so pleased to flash on your finger, the carpets you so eagerly show to our visitors at home—and many more things I can't even think about right now—they're all made available to you because a lot of unfortunate children were denied the opportunity to go to school, and had to work in a factory instead. The ones that worked in our homes are not the only victims. You're happy to buy fast fashion, but unhappy that people are bragging about having young servants for housework. The problem is bigger and more complex than you think. Yes, we don't see little children working in the households in Australia, America, or other developed countries, but even they are consuming things made by those children. We can only speculate about how many children must have lost their lives in the Bangladeshi factory fire. They weren't working in homes, but making clothes for people to wear in wealthy countries. How is that any different? So, my dear, unless you're going to do something about it, stop labeling people as insensitive or morally inferior to you. It's driving me insane."

"Look, I never said India has the monopoly on all social evils, but I've lived there, and experienced them at a personal level. And you're right, I never do anything. I just harp about it and think that I'm morally superior because of that. I'm also guilty of taking you down the farcical trenches of my despair over the poor and underprivileged. I'll call Tulika and apologize as soon as we're home." She took him by surprise. It was unusual for her to close any battles until she made them into lengthy wars. She was probably tired and wanted to end the topic quickly. They couldn't reach home fast enough.

"Rohini, there was a letter for you in your mailbox, all the way from India." Rachel knocked at her office door. "And I got it for you!" She waved the cream-colored envelope with the handwriting she very well knew.

"Dear Rohini,

This is an unfortunate father asking for his daughter's forgiveness. I don't know how to atone for my sins, if atonement is at all possible. Looking at your innocent face day after day and pretending that nothing happened, wasn't easy. But that's exactly what I did. Now here I am, after all those years, asking you to help me get out of my living hell.

I didn't have to read your journal to know how I hurt you, but it gave words to my crime. All this time, I lived each day thinking you would ask me why you had to be the victim of your own protector. I'm still dreading that question, as I don't have the answer.

Your mother thinks of me as the most unfortunate child, because I lost one father when I was too young to remember anything, and, didn't know about another one until it was too late. Gopal called me and took the opportunity to tell me the origin of my birth. Samraj, my biological father, died last week.

You and I would agree that your mother is wrong. You're the most unfortunate child, not me. My tragedy is understandable, unlike yours. I know there is no justification, no defense, and no atonement.

I can only hope that you find some peace in this letter and try to forgive me.

Your father."

"No, it doesn't give me peace to know that you've dreaded my question, that you probably knew I wouldn't have the courage to ask. There is no closure for me, ever," Rohini said out loud, sunk in the chair, and let go of her emotions that had been bottled up for more than twenty years. She had once tried to tell her mother about being violated by him, but she was denied any compassion. Rohini was afraid of him and had been embarrassed for herself since then, and that letter in her hand felt surreal. *What was she going to do with it? Was she going to reply? How awkward would it be when they spoke on the phone next time? Will he ask her if she got the letter? Was she going to say yes, or just deny ever getting it?*

Samraj died a few weeks ago, and no one called to let her know. She wondered if anyone from her family attended the funeral. She could only guess.

"Ajit, let's go out for dinner tonight, just the two of us. There's something I want to share with you." She left a voice message on his phone at work.

"Good morning, Sister, are you sleeping already? Oh, of course, I forgot you sleep in the evening when we start to get into action." Deepak was on the phone.

"Yes, my brother, if evening means ten at night. We do, in fact, sleep quite early, but that's never stopped you from calling me anyways. How are you? I'd been meaning to call you, since we're planning our India trip for this summer in December, I mean, your winter." Waking up by a phone call wasn't something Rohini enjoyed, but her brothers never called at a convenient time.

"Your India trip sounds wonderful! Riya also wanted to talk to you about something. I don't remember the details, but I think it has to do with a special friend. Do you have any idea?"

"No, but I can guess who that special friend could be. Tell her I'll call her tomorrow. Is that *really* why you called me at this time?"

"Hmm. No, not really. It's a matter that's been brewing up here, and I thought it might be important for you to know. You're probably aware that Swati *Bua* ("father's sister") is still fighting the legal battle against the donor's son."

"Yes, Mom told me something along those lines. Any progress there?"

"Not exactly progress, but some development that is bothersome. Manoj *Bhaiya* has become her strong opponent, and he doesn't want that school to reopen. Has she discussed anything with you?"

"No, unfortunately not. I never got in touch with her after Raghu *Kaka*'s funeral in Narayanpur. Tell me what's going on. No, I lied. I did get an e-mail from my ex-boss at the law firm about *Bua* calling him for help. Frankly, I didn't pay much attention, and it went away. My boss didn't say what help she was looking for, and I didn't follow up on that either. Do you think I should have?"

"You probably should've, but we understand you are superbusy with your work and family. I know you care deeply about *Baba* and his school, so I thought I should let you know that *Bua* is trying her best to keep his dreams alive. We meet with her every now and then, and slowly, are getting to know her better. Honestly, she's the prodigal daughter. I mean, who does so much for others?

She's looking after not only her mother but also those five girls she unofficially adopted after the school was closed. She's sustaining them by juggling a job in a hospital, and running small private tutorial classes. She probably never sleeps." Deepak's praise for Swati was making her quite uneasy.

"Yeah, so you are calling me late at night to tell me how great our Swati *Bua* is?"

"No, *Didi*, not at all. I'm telling you about *Bua* because she is dedicated to something *Baba* gave his life for, and I thought you were passionate about it, too."

"Well, I didn't say I'm not passionate about *Baba's* dream. I get it alright, but could you tell me why suddenly it's Swati *Bua* this and Swati *Bua* that? I mean, when did she become this superwoman you're gushing about? What's she going around and asking help for? Does she want money to open the school?"

"*Didi*, she's been fighting that battle since the donor's son and Manoj colluded to shut down the school, to open a private engineering college. You remember, she was worried about where the kids might end up, and also for those poor girls whose parents didn't want them back. Luckily, she found a supporter in a good lawyer who's helping her pro bono. He said he knows you from his college days in Delhi. He might have had a crush on you, and could be wanting to impress you. Ha! Just kidding! Whatever the reason, he's been very good. We meet with him sometimes too. Great guy. Do you remember Sohail Khanna?" Of course she did, and yes, he did have a crush on her in college. She was blushing now.

"Sohail, huh! He'll be good at it. So what more does she want? Is there a plan for filing a petition, and what do you think I could do from here?"

"You don't need to do anything at this stage. We are trying our best to settle this outside the court, but also preparing for the worst. *Bua* has made friends at the local newspaper and TV stations that have promised to help. I think we'll need all the support we can get, but, frankly, I don't think she cares about the power of the people we're up against. She knows they're connected with the mafia and politicians. But driven by her passion for the school and her father's dream, she doesn't even entertain the possibility of not getting what she wants. I'm a little concerned. You know what it's like, right?"

"I do. Be careful. Don't get carried away and rally behind her. She's got nothing to lose, and everything to gain. Anyways, you're adults and grown up enough to know what's good or bad for you. I'm just giving you advice. I hope that makes sense."

"*Didi,* you really surprise me sometimes. I thought you were passionate about the school, and wanted to do great things for children. I grew up seeing you being the champion of education for all, but it seems you aren't bothered anymore. Perhaps you have a lot to lose and nothing to gain. You better get some sleep. Talk to you later." Deepak's disappointment hurt Rohini. He was right. She didn't even know what she was passionate about anymore.

"OK, good night, and keep me posted." Ignoring his remarks and pretending everything was fine, she ended the call. She dug in to bed, knowing well that sleep was far away.

"Is everything alright, dear? Do you want to talk about that phone call?" Ajit was sleeping next to her, but he was awake enough to know something was going on.

"Yes, everything is fine. You sleep. I'll go get a snack. I'm just a little hungry." She had a great stress appetite.

She mulled over a tub of ice cream. *How should it make her feel? Was she really concerned about Swati's welfare, or did she dread that she might become a hero? Once again, no one asked her for help, but was she even willing to? If she did, there was still time. Or did she have a lot to lose?* It was much easier to just talk about social issues and make moral arguments. If attaining a high ground was the only objective, she was almost there. *Why bother? Just eat some more ice cream, go to sleep, and things will go away as they always have.*

"Mum, I don't have clothes for India. We need to do some shopping. Can you give me your credit card number? I'll buy them online." Somya was standing in front of her wardrobe the next morning.

"*Didi*, can you buy me some clothes, too? I haven't got anything to wear." Sohum was standing behind her, looking in the exact same direction.

"This is my wardrobe. Why don't you look in yours and see? Didn't Mum buy you heaps last month?"

"No, I want new ones."

"Mum, could I use your credit card or not?"

"Seriously, Somya, wait for a minute, will you?" Rohini was downstairs, booking flights from Mumbai to Bokaro. Everything else was booked, and they were set to leave next month. It was going to be two years since their last visit, which was too long, as she had been reminded by her mother-in-law in every phone call for the last six months.

"I think I need new clothes for the trip as well. What do you say? Ajit, what's the matter? Is there anything interesting going on in the world, my newsaholic husband?"

"Wait a second, Rohini, will you?" He snapped at her, and returned to intently looking at the laptop.

"Sure, take your time. I'm going upstairs to see what they're up to."

"So, have you decided what you would like to buy?" Rohini peeked behind Somya and Sohum in the guest room, where they browsed their favorite clothing store online.

"Can I buy all the clothes here, Mum?" Sohum asked.

"No, you can't buy all of them. Just four should be enough. Let's see what your sister is looking at. Did you find anything you like, Somya?"

"No, I'm still looking, Mom. Can you help me, please?" Somya was deeply engaged in the shop's online catalogue.

"Mom, Dad told me we're also going to Kerala this time to stay in a boat house. That sounds supercool. But I was looking at the temperature, and it's all over the place. I need winter clothes for some places and summer clothes for others, making it so difficult to decide." She deeply distressed.

It was going to be a fun trip.

"Guess what? *Didi* showed me our boathouse. It has lots of blue curtains. She said we'll live in the river. Will there be sharks in it?"

"When did that happen? Oh, God, why didn't you call us before? No, we're not that far, Deepak. Shit! What now? Where is her mother? What? Narayanpur? When? God, I don't even know how to react. Yes, I saw the news website, but it's full of rubbish by that sleazy politician. Where is the body? Yes, she is here, upstairs with the kids. I don't know yet. Let me talk to her. I'll call you back. Please tell me if you need anything. OK?" Ajit was shouting on the phone.

Whose body was he talking about, with whom?

"Rohini, could you come downstairs, please?" He barely finished the sentence before she stood next to him.

"What happened? Why are you shaking?" She was beginning to get nervous, looking at his pale face and unusually jittery posture. He didn't reply but just turned the laptop toward her. It was put on a local news channel in Mumbai. The newsreader was reporting on big local news, and a screen was scrolling down with snippets of other less important ones. There it appeared in a few seconds: "Swati Dubey, the director of *Damyanti Baal Vikaas* School, was challenging the opening of an engineering college in the same building . . . the school was illegally run . . . no foul play is suspected in her death . . ." She looked at him, wanting to know what was happening. *Swati Dubey was? No foul play in her death?*

"What the hell are they saying? I can't read it anymore, and I don't want to." She collapsed in to the couch, staring at the ceiling, as if the laptop just sucked the life out of her. After a few minutes of her frozen state, she suddenly got out of the couch and started walking out of the room when Ajit held her hand.

"Rohini, no point denying what's happening. You can't run away. We can't run away now. Your aunty has been slaughtered by that corrupt politician, so he could make loads of money, and deny innocent children their chance for a better future. And look at his guts! The sleaze is going around, spreading lies about his noble work of cleansing the school, and establishing a 'true house of education.' He just said to the news reporter that your aunty was running a prostitution ring out of that building, and one of its teacher's arrest for sexually assaulting the children was clear proof. I haven't seen a worse human being in my life. Listen to him. He's still going on." He made her sit on his lap while she blankly looked at the screen.

"I'm sad that Ms. Dubey passed away in an accident, and I feel terrible for her poor mother, who is now left alone. May God give her peace! Such an unfortunate mother she is, to have given birth to a child of such bad character. But then, ladies and gentlemen, she's not a role model for a strong woman herself. As many of us know, she had lured an older, married Brahmin man into marrying her. That school has always been run by morally corrupt people who perpetrated crime of a level you cannot even imagine. I know what was happening behind those walls in the name of 'education for the poor and underprivileged.' You would remember the news of one of their teachers molesting the children, and I don't even want to give you anymore examples. But I promise you, it's going to be over, and soon there'll be a world-class engineering college for our youth, the future of our great country. You may know Ms. Dubey was going to file a petition against us, with the support of some evil-spirited lawyers and so-called social workers. Well, they can all rest now and let us do the good work. All I seek is your blessings. Thank you, and God bless you."

"What a load of crap!" Ajit fumed.

"It isn't an accident! Not an accident!" she screamed in despair and wrapped her hands around his shoulders.

"Oh, shit!" Before Ajit could react, she had passed out.

"Mom, Mom! You OK?" Somya came, running downstairs, and stopped outside the office. Sohum followed her and tried to peep in.

"What happened to Mom? Did she hurt herself, Daddy? I've got some Band-Aids, the Superman ones." Sohum reached into his pocket and tried to get close to Rohini.

"She'll be fine. Thanks for offering your Band-Aids, but she doesn't need them right now, sweetheart. Why don't you go upstairs and play with Sis for a while, and Mom and I'll meet you there soon."

"Somya, please take him upstairs. Mom will be fine. She's just a little upset. I'll tell you what happened later, but, first, I need to make sure she recovers."

"Sure, Dad, Sohum, let's go," Somya said, wiping her tears away. They went upstairs without any protest. Ajit smiled at the little people's understanding and composure. Adults could learn from them.

"May I come in?" Rohini knocked at her boss's door.

"Hey! Since when did you start asking my permission to come in? Welcome back." Marge got out of the chair and hugged her.

"Oh, dear, look at you. It seems you haven't slept for ages. You didn't have to come in today. Take another day off if you like. Ajit called me that day from the hospital and told me about your aunt's accident. I'm so sorry for your loss. He told me how fragile you were at that time, so I didn't want to disturb you. He was so apologetic, as if it was his fault. God bless him. He's a lovely man. Here, at work, Michael came in to see me soon after you left, wondering if he should be the project manager for the Pilbara Council work. He was, of course, only concerned about the work, and was willing to help." Marge chuckled.

"Of course," both said together, Marge laughed, and Rohini gave a subdued smile.

"Something is still bothering you. Am I right? Your smile is such a giveaway."

"And, of course, you're correct."

"So what is it?"

"Maybe Michael should take over the project."

"What do you mean? I thought you loved working on it. But if that's what you want, then it's fine by me. Phew, I thought you were going to say something else."

"No, it's not really the project. I wish it was that simple."

Rohini's throat was getting dry. She reached out for a bottle of water from the coffee table and closed the door on her way back to the desk.

"Marge, I have unfinished business back in India, and I've got to be there." She took a sip of water and looked in her eyes.

"So you want more days off? How much?"

"It'll be longer than days. Maybe years, or forever. I'm not sure yet."

"Goodness, what's going on with you? I don't mean to poke my nose in your personal matters, but if you wish, I would like to know how I could help, if at all. Just know that I'll always support you, and I'll do my best to accommodate your needs. You know I'd hate to lose you."

"Do you really want to know? We could be here all day."

"I do have a day for you, if that's what it takes." She dialed the phone.

"Linda, please cancel my meetings for the day. Yes, the lunch as well."

"I'm all yours, now." She smiled and looked at Rohini with expectant eyes. She knew it wasn't going to be a fairytale, but she was ready for it.

"My aunt's death shook me and changed my world. She didn't die in a random accident, as you might have heard. She was murdered by those who couldn't stand her guts."

"Oh my Lord! I'm so shocked to hear that! But what're you going to do about it?"

"I don't know how to tell you exactly what I'm going to do, as I'm still trying to make sense of it. But I know one thing for sure. I've been a coward and hypocrite all this while, and I feel responsible for a few people whose childhoods may be snatched away from them, if I don't do something soon."

"I wouldn't call you a coward, or a hypocrite. You're one of the bravest and most honest people I've ever come across. You stand up for the right thing, without hesitation and let people know what you think. You have a big heart. Why beat yourself up unnecessarily?"

"Yes, I do talk about the right things, and argue over what I think is wrong. But that's all I do, Marge. I haven't done anything meaningful so far. My aunt gave her life, working for children's education, and my grandfather devoted his entire life to that cause. Why go so far? You volunteer your time, helping children with their education too. All I do is perform greatly in debates over social issues. I always have grand ideals for how to fix them, but have I done my bit? Not even remotely. You would have noticed how keen I am to gain a high ground on things like education for all, child labor, prejudice against anyone and anything, and myriads of other issues I seem to champion."

"Well, it doesn't surprise me to see you promote those values, given how highly educated you are, and the charitable family you come from. I remember you telling me about your grandfather's legacy. I've also witnessed you shredding Geetika to pieces when she complained about life in Australia without *servants*. You put her in the right place when she moaned about how scarce and expensive they were becoming in India because of the 'flu of education.' I was so proud of you."

"You've seen only what I wanted you to see, and known only what I wanted you to know. What you don't know is that I brought a young girl for housework and babysitting at my house in Mumbai, and I treated her like a piece of dirt. Even though I had every intention of educating her, frankly, I never tried hard enough. I was too wrapped up in making sure my own child was looked after well to worry about her. So, you see, that's my record on child labor and education for all. When my aunt was being kicked out of the school, and needed to take care of five young girls, I dreaded she might ask for help, and you know what? I was relieved when she didn't. I couldn't even be bothered to find out how she managed afterward. The least I could do when we left for Perth, after barely a few months, was to offer my house, but I never did."

"But that's understandable to some extent . . ."

"Wait, there's more.

"I was full of rage when my brother told me that they were in touch with her and supported her efforts. Why did it bother me so much? Probably because I thought I was the one with the big heart, big dreams, and grand ideals, but she was about to get the credit. I met with her mother at her funeral who was grieving for her daughter, but with great pride. She was glad her daughter gave her life doing what was right. I'm not sure my mother can say the same about me."

"So you want to go back and make sure those girls are taken care of?" Marge gulped and tried to understand where things were.

"Yes, that too. I don't know exactly what I need to do, but I cannot let my aunt's life go in vain. I've lived with the stories of my grandfather who believed that most social issues, if not all, could be fixed by education. I believe in that too, but it took me very long to realize that I haven't done anything to help anyone. If not now, when? I want to go back and figure it out. Here's my resignation letter. I'm sorry, Marge." Rohini took out a yellow envelope with "Marge Brown" written on it.

"Guess I'll have to start looking for a job in India, then?" Marge said, trying to make it light. They laughed after an awkward pause.

"Lunch at my favorite place? I'm craving Turkish." Marge knew Rohini would never say no to food.

The Beginning

Rohini got off the journey into the past with the sound of a car stopping in front of her.

Ajit opened the door, and Anjali came out of the car with a little boy clinging on to her. She looked slightly different from how Rohini had imagined her—attractive, tall, and beaming with confidence. Of course, she hadn't imagined that smile, having snatched it from her so mercilessly.

Rohini's trepidation about coming face-to-face with Anjali made the wait seem a lot longer than it was, and she nervously waited to see her up close. After what seemed like years, Anjali was standing in front of her with the boy, who was holding her hand, and looking up at Rohini.

"*Didi*, I can't believe I'm seeing you again. I never thought this day would ever come." Rohini hesitated to hug Anjali, but her excitement relaxed her tense nerves, and she opened her arms for an embrace long due.

"I know, it has been such a long time, I'm so glad you came. Believe me, I always asked my parents about you. You look so . . . so . . . ladylike! And who is this handsome young man?"

"Oh, you're embarrassing me, *Didi*. I look nothing compared to you, and you look even better now. Is there something special in the water in Australia? Where are your children? Can I meet with them? Somya must be a big girl now. I still keep this photo of her and me when she was little and I was pushing her at the swing. Remember? You took that picture. Do you want to see?" Anjali dug into her handbag, took out a wallet, and flipped it open. There it was—the day, so fresh in her memory. It was a beautiful picture of Somya in a swing in their apartment complex's playground in Mumbai and Anjali pushing her.

"*Didi,* are you crying? Oh, no, I didn't mean to hurt you. It is such a special picture that I always kept close to me. I really am sorry if that made you sad." Anjali got a little perplexed by her tears.

"Who, me? No, I'm not . . . Well, yes, these are the tears that I've been meaning to shed for a long time. I haven't forgotten all the cruel and mean things I did to you." She let them roll down her cheeks.

"I don't think you've done anything wrong. I mean, I had the disease that you or Ajit sir or Somya could catch, and anyone in your position would have done the same thing. My father said bad things to your family, and I apologize for that, but if you keep crying like this, I'll have to leave. Please stop, and tell me about your life in Australia." Ajit picked up a box of tissues from the corner table and handed it over to her.

"Anjali, is he your son? He's so cute, but he doesn't really look like you. Maybe he looks like his dad. I'm guessing, of course. Sorry for asking these silly questions. You can choose to say nothing. Absolutely nothing." He smiled awkwardly at Anjali.

"Ajit sir, no problem. You can ask me any questions. I'm feeling awful seeing *Didi* cry."

"I know, but she'll be fine. She feels bad about what happened and never stopped thinking about it. It's only natural for her to react this way after seeing you."

"I'm fine now. Sorry about that." Rohini wiped away her tears and turned around.

"You know both our parents are here too. I don't know why, but I find it amazing that they came together in the same car, and survived the journey without any fall outs." That was Ajit's way of making it light, and once again, he succeeded.

"So ladies, we better go inside too. A lot of people are already here," he said.

"Yes, let's go now. Anjali, I'm sure you know why you're here?" Rohini asked.

"Of course, to see the inauguration of your school, *Didi*." Anjali flashed her signature smile.

"Really? That's all? Weren't you told who the special guest was, and why you were invited?"

"Yes, that's all I know, if I remember correctly. Your father's driver came to my house and told my mother that you were opening a school in town, and it would be nice if I could come to see that. My mother, still harboring a grudge over my coming back from Mumbai sooner than she'd expected, decided not to tell me anything. Luckily, my brother heard about it and sent me a message. My in-laws were surprised at the invitation to a school opening, and asked me if I was going to get a job there as a teacher. They were worried that I might leave them, and move to Bokaro. I had to console them that I wasn't planning on doing any such thing. Since I'm the sole caretaker for them after my husband's death last year in a road accident, I understand their paranoia." She stopped immediately, as the little boy came running from the lobby and hugged her.

"Oh, how terrible! I didn't even know when you got married. I would've loved to come to your wedding. Sorry, I don't know what I'm saying. I'm so sad to hear that Anjali. Do you want to sit down and settle the little one before we go inside? Ajit, you go ahead. We'll be there soon," she said to him as he was walking in front of them. He looked back, gave them a smile, and kept going toward the hall.

"It was my destiny. What can I do?" Anjali said as they sat on the sofa in the hallway.

"Pawan, my husband, was a good man, and we were happy together. He treated me as his equal, and had a dream for both of us to work as teachers in the village school. He was employed as a taxi driver while studying to get his teaching qualification. One day, he was waiting at a street corner for passengers when he heard a woman's scream. It was coming from a house that had smoke bellowing out the door. He ran toward the house, and before he could realize what was happening, he saw a baby crawling out of the front door and about to go on the busy street. He grabbed the baby and looked inside, where a big ball of fire seemed to be in a trance. It was a woman in flames, the baby's mother. She died in the hospital the next day, leaving the baby with Pawan."

"How did she catch on fire?"

"You can guess what happened."

"Her husband or in-laws planned her murder, and made it look like an accident?"

"Sadly, your guess is absolutely correct. Her husband had let the gas leak from the stove before leaving for work, and as soon as the wife came in and lit the stove, she was caught up in the explosion."

"I hope he's in jail now."

"Yes, he's rotting there. We haven't been able to eliminate the human greed for money, but at least the strict dowry laws are helping to put the perpetrators where they belong. Most of them anyways."

"Pawan was very upset, and couldn't get himself to part with the baby. After the husband went to jail, the baby's aunty happily agreed to let us have him forever. We adopted him, and he's right here in front of you. Meet Guddu, the little devil." Anjali bent and looked over Guddu, who was hanging on her legs. They both smiled at each other.

"He's adorable, and so lucky to have you. It's amazing how much had happened, and I didn't know a thing. You've seen a lot in life, much earlier than I did for sure. And you mentioned that both you and your husband wanted to become teachers. Were you planning to study at that time?"

"Oh, I forgot to tell you. After I came back from Mumbai and recovered from the rashes, I told my mother that I was going to school, and would no longer work in anyone's house. I knew you wanted me to do just that. If I went to work anywhere else, I wouldn't have been able to study. My father, of course, wanted me to work so he could drink every night. Luckily, my mother fought her way out and used the money you had let her keep in the bank on my education. So you see, *Didi*, you made me study, after all." Anjali held Rohini's left pinky finger and curled it up with her own.

"So I did." There were no words to describe Anjali's greatness. She made her feel very little and very big at the same time. She wasn't surprised by her large heart, but was still amazed at the extent of its purity. *Where did she get such grace and maturity from?*

"OK, let's go, ladies. Everyone is waiting for you. We should start the program now." Ajit hesitated to intervene during their intense conversation.

Rohini was eager to get out of the huge ocean of gratitude she found herself drowning in, and was glad for Ajit's interruption. She stood up immediately, and Anjali followed her toward the small auditorium.

"Anjali, you're the special guest. That means you'll light the lamp, unveil two portraits, announce the official start of the school, and, only if you want to, say a few words. That's all. We haven't made it too formal." Rohini gave her quick instructions about her role as they rushed inside. The auditorium was abuzz with children playing around, and adults trying to keep them in one place. As Anjali, Rohini, and Ajit walked in with Guddu, the noise level went down gradually. There was complete silence when Rohini waved at them, and greeted them in *Namaste*. She was a little nervous about being responsible for the dreams and expectations of so many children and their families. *Was she right in thinking she could build a school, and make their dreams come true?*

"*Namaste,* everyone, we're gathered here today for the inauguration of your school, which I hope becomes your favorite place and, hopefully, your second home. This lady standing next to me is Anjali, our special guest today. She'll help us light the holy lamp, and unveil two portraits to dedicate this school to the great people who have inspired me. After that, we'll go out to the playground and have some fun. You'll also join us in eating lots of food afterwards. How does that sound?" If the roar of claps and giggles were any indication, the plan had no flaws.

Anjali lit multiple oil lamps in a tall brass stand with a candle, and pulled tiny curtains to unveil the portraits. Her hands were shaking, and she was giggling nervously. When Rohini tried to give her the microphone to speak, she waved her hands and apologized. She could only take so much of the limelight in a day. Being there as a special guest would take a lifetime to sink in. She wasn't ready for anymore.

Rohini's *Baba* and Swati were smiling from their portraits. They seemed happy to be there.

"So, should we declare our school open now?" Rohini asked, and received another thunderous applause from her very excited audience.

"But before we go out and have fun together, I would like to tell you about the two people you see here in these portraits." Rohini paused to gauge the room. Everyone went silent, and her family looked straight at her with questions written on their faces. She knew what those questions were, but didn't feel obliged to offer an explanation. She surprised herself with that thought. She was free at last from the need to please.

"These two people are the inspirations behind this school. They are my *Baba*, and his daughter. I never saw him in person, but got to know him through his stories told by my grandmother. *Baba* worked to make education available to all, regardless of their class or caste, and *Bua* followed his steps and gave her life for the same cause. They are the reason this school is here today. Someday, I'll write a book about them, and you'll get a chance to know them well." She barely managed to finish the last sentence before being showered with applause from the audience. Her father's hands started the first clap. *Could she ask for more?*

"Anjali, may I ask you to grace this school with your service? You'll be the reason for many of these children to come here every day. I know you don't want to go away from your lonely in-laws, but what if they could come with you and live here? I'll provide for your accommodation close to school. Think about it. If you want, I can also . . ." Anjali put her hand on Rohini's and pressed lightly.

"*Didi*, you don't need to convince me. I'll be honored to be of any help. You have done so much for these children. The least I could do is work here with them. I'm sure my in-laws will understand. Whether they come here and live with me or not, I'll let them decide. Oh, look, Guddu is already busy playing with his new friends in the sandpit. I guess it'll be difficult to keep him off from this paradise you have created." Anjali's words were washing away Rohini's guilt, slowly but surely. The two women watched everyone take their place at the food stalls, in the playground, on the benches and around the flower beds. They had smiling faces— innocent, non-judgmental, and perhaps forgiving—on behalf of all those deprived of their right to education.

"Look who's here!" shouted Ajit, who was coming toward the sandpit, and Sohum was holding his hand. Rohini and Anjali were sitting on the bench next to the sandpit. There was someone else with him. As they came closer, Rohini was astounded. *Was he really who she thought?*

"Hello, my dear gorgeous woman!" Sohail gave a peck on Rohini's cheek.

"Look at you, handsome as ever! Sohail, this is Anjali. Anjali, Sohail is my classmate from law school. As you can see, he never stopped trying to flirt with me."

"*Namaste*, Sohail *Bhaiya*." Anjali folded her hands for him.

"Anjali, there you are. I've heard a lot about you, all good things, of course. Glad to see you," Sohail said, smiling.

"Rohini, you have done a great job, my dear. Your parents must be so proud."

"Her husband is very proud too," Ajit chuckled.

"No, the wife is proud to have such a husband. Really, I never said this out loud, but Ajit saved me from every negative force that caught me in its grip, along what's been a long journey. Whatever little I've done so far, has been possible only because of him." She put her arms around his waist, and glowed with joy.

"My, my, this is some love. I'm unnecessarily trying my luck here. Don't I have any chance, Rohini?"

"No, not in this life."

"Well, I better reserve the next one soon."

"Sohail, all are taken."

They laughed out loud.

"I get it and I apologize for even trying, and sorry also for missing the inauguration today. My train was late, which shouldn't really surprise me, but to add icing on the cake, a very efficient pickpocket at your beloved Bokaro station made my day."

"Oh, I'm so sorry to hear that. What an icing on the cake!," Rohini said flirtatiously.

"On the positive side, though, we had a small win last week. The high court granted the appeal to admit our case to prove continuous occupation of the school building. That small win paves the way for claiming ownership of the entire precinct. We could do it if you are willing to pursue the case. I'll be there, of course."

"Sohail, look at these children. I see hope in their eyes. Would I be willing to see many more of that? You bet!"

She felt true happiness, and smiled from the bottom of her heart after a long long time.

Dear Father,

I got your letter three years ago but didn't know what to say in reply. I know you must have been wondering all along.

As I write this, I'm thinking about all the good things you have done for me and all the bad ones you shouldn't have. I believe, like many of us, that the purest form of love is between a parent and a child. By becoming a parent, one learns to love *unconditionally*. However, it is also a universal truth that we are, after all, human and capable of making mistakes. Until recently, I blamed myself for being at the receiving end of your fury and abuse. It has been a long journey, fighting away the feelings of inadequacy, self-loathing, fear, and shame. One would have thought I'd never want to see anyone else in that fight, let alone be the one to put them there. But that's exactly what I did. I was trusted unequivocally by Anjali, but I betrayed her. I was so obsessed with my child that I didn't give any thought to what I was doing to someone else's. Despite wanting to be a giver, I ended up becoming a dream snatcher.

Although the two aren't similar events, I can relate to both Anjali for her pain, and you for your yearning to be forgiven.

It wasn't easy to seek forgiveness from Anjali, but it was even harder to forgive myself. She was graceful, as always, in showing me how to embrace others with their faults. She also taught me how to let others have grace in seeking forgiveness.

I forgive you. It's your turn to forgive yourself.

I choose to no longer let my life be defined by the wrongs done to me and the wrongs I did to others.

People always said I was your favorite child. Now is the time to cherish that status.

With love from a fortunate daughter,
Rohini

The End